CLOSING TIME

ISBN: 978-1-68313-102-1

Cover photograph from the collection of Karen Staton Farmer. Other photos used with permission of *Fort Smith Times Record* and *Van Buren Press Argus Courier*, Karen Staton Farmer, and Ruth Staton Morrison. Pencil drawing of Rick Anderson by Matthew Dennis Wilson, with permission.

Cover and interior design by Kelsey Rice

First Edition
Printed and bound in the USA

CLOSING TIME

A TRUE STORY OF ROBBERY AND RUTHLESS DOUBLE MURDER THAT SHOOK A SMALL TOWN

by

ANITA PADDOCK

Pen-L Publishing
Fayetteville, Arkansas
Pen-L.com

BOOKS BY ANITA PADDOCK

BLIND RAGE: A true story of sin, sex, and murder in a small Arkansas Town

CLOSING TIME: A true story of robbery and ruthless double murder that shook a small town

*For Anita Lynn Patton: my namesake niece,
dearest friend, and greatest literary supporter,
whom I've adored all her life.*

"Now this case actually starts prior to September 10th, 1980, when two people get together up at Rogers, Arkansas, to decide that they are going to rob a jewelry store located at the Cloverleaf Plaza in Van Buren."

– RON FIELDS, Prosecuting Attorney, Circuit Court of Sebastian County

CHAPTER ONE

September was always hot in Arkansas. Even though the calendar signaled the coming of fall and schools opened for a new school year, the oppressive heat dragged on for Arkansans long wearied of hot weather. Schools tried to fight the weather by starting early, around 7:30, and dismissing shortly after lunch. It helped some. Teachers reported that there were few discipline problems in classrooms cooled by fans on stands.

"The students are just too hot to act up."

Van Buren—a small town of eight thousand across the Arkansas River from the second-largest city in Arkansas, Fort Smith—was sweltering in that summer of 1980. The temperature on July 13th had reached 108, and the hot spell would continue on through the middle of September. The humidity stayed at ninety percent and kept ladies' hair frizzed and men's shirt collars wet. Tempers were short, and moods were bad. Everyone said so.

Air conditioners whirred, rarely catching the signal that the desired temperature had been reached on the thermostat. It was the busiest time of the year for service calls for McBride Plumbing and Electric, and seldom were people pleased when told they were sixth on the list.

1

On that 10th morning of the month, a Wednesday, at the Cloverleaf Plaza Shopping Center on US Highway 64 east of downtown Van Buren, business owners and managers were arriving. Friendly greetings were called out, and most carried the morning newspaper and maybe a sack lunch or midmorning snack.

Kenneth Staton, dressed in a short sleeved white shirt and black trousers, parked his light-blue '77 Mercury in the parking lot beside a light pole, saving spots close to the door of his jewelry store for his customers. Staton Jewelry was nicely positioned between two stores: Hunt's Department Store and Gennell's Dress Shop. The store officially opened at 9:30, but he liked to arrive early to get started on his watch repair before customers arrived or the phone rang. A big part of his business was jewelry and watch repair, and it was tedious but profitable work.

Kent, as everyone called him—except his wife, Ruth, whom he called Ruthie—was crippled with rheumatoid arthritis and had been since he was a young married man. Confined to a wheelchair for some twenty years, he'd learned the watch repair business from a correspondence course. After long stays in hospitals for treatments and surgeries that didn't work, he had finally found relief, ironically, in a car wreck that broke his hip. Following the surgery to replace that hip, he had been able to use arm crutches for the last ten years.

After years of hard work, during which he earned the title of jeweler, he and his wife had operated a small jewelry store in Fort Smith and Ozark. He was now able to do what he always wanted to do: support his family. His four daughters, beauties like their mom, had graduated from Fort Smith schools, and now two of the four—Karen, the oldest, and Suzanne, the youngest—worked beside him in their Van Buren store at the Cloverleaf Shopping Center.

The second-oldest, Janet, was married and lived in Paris, Texas. She and her husband, Tommy, had two children: Jon and Sara. Elaine (Staton) Barham and her husband, Bill, lived in Van Buren, near her two sisters. Their son, Ben, a happy twenty-two-month-old, was the only grandchild close by, so he was spoiled, especially by his aunts, who saw him nearly every day.

Kenneth Staton seldom complained or let on to others that he was in pain, but Ruth knew better. A furrowed brow, a grimace, told her when the pain was especially bad.

Despite his handicap, and with determination few people possess, he owned a successful business, and with the help of his wife and daughters who clerked in the store, they looked forward to the coming holiday season. The Christmas merchandise had arrived, and Kent was confident that this would be their best year yet.

He looked at his watch and made a mental note that he'd have nearly an hour before Suzanne arrived to help him open. He then slid the key into the lock on the front door of Staton's Jewelry for the last time.

KENNETH AND RUTH, BEFORE MARRIAGE

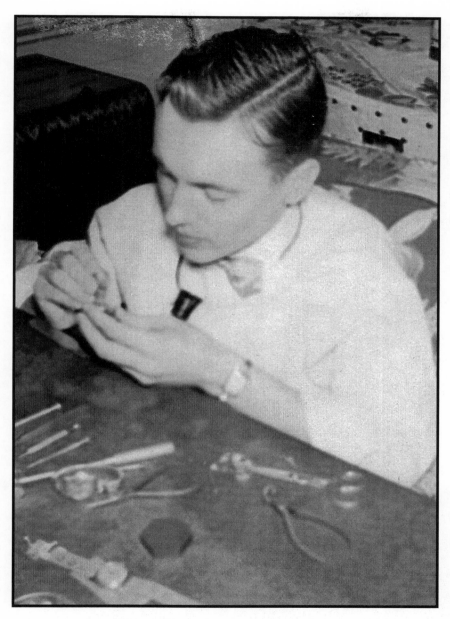

KENNETH, LEARNING HIS TRADE

MARCH 1952 / Karen

KENNETH AND RUTH WITH KAREN

FOUR STATON GIRLS FROM LEFT TO RIGHT:
SUZANNE, JANET, KAREN, AND ELAINE

Kenneth at work in back room of Cloverleaf Plaza store

KENNETH AND SUZANNE AT CHRISTMAS

CHAPTER TWO

While Kenneth Staton was opening his jewelry store, two men—a twenty-three-year-old with dark, shaggy hair and a tall man in his mid-thirties with fuzzy, dyed blond hair—sat on twin beds in the rundown, cheap Terry Motel, located on Midland Boulevard, just across the river from Van Buren. The room, number 18, had been rented by the older man under the name of Damon Peterson with a Georgia address. The motorcycle on which he and the younger guy were riding was listed as owned by Rick Anderson, and it was licensed in Florida.

Condensation from the window air conditioner dripped water on an already saturated orange shag carpet that could use a good cleaning. The air, only slightly cool, hung heavy with cigar smoke, soured beer, and Air Wick. The outside door was once painted black, but scuff marks and indentations from angry heel prints had taken their toll. Grime covered the only window, where someone had drawn a heart with *Gerald loves Louise* inside it.

Midland Boulevard was full of cheap hotels and bars with names like The Branding Iron, The Flamingo, the Oasis, and The Glass Hat. Because Van Buren was in a dry county, and Fort Smith wasn't, Midland was the quickest route to pick up a six-pack of Bud or a bottle of Jack

Daniel's. Some customers parked on the side of the stores, hoping not to be seen entering the establishments preached against on Sunday mornings, while some muttered a curse and hoped that someday they would be able to buy a beer in Van Buren.

These two men at the Terry Motel had met less than a week earlier at a campground near Horseshoe Bend on Beaver Lake in Rogers: north on Highway 71 and north again on Highway 94.

Rick Anderson, the young guy, and his girlfriend, Chantina Ginn, had arrived at the campgrounds after the carnival they worked for had closed in Topeka, Kansas. They had some time to kill before the carnival opened again in Fort Smith, Arkansas, so they followed some other carnies to Beaver Lake to camp out. One man, Pete Hubbard, had offered them his camper to use at night in campsite 1-9, but they argued because Hubbard called Rick "pussy whipped" for offering to bring Chantina a towel when she asked for one after swimming in the lake.

This argument over a man being kind and polite to his girlfriend caused Hubbard to pack up, leaving Rick and Chantina high and dry.

Damon Peterson and his wife, Loralei, registered at the campground after the carnival bunch, and they were assigned to the camp site next to Rick and Chantina at 1-10. Rick and Chantina were poorly equipped for camping. Their only possessions were sleeping bags and his prized dark-blue Harley with a sissy bar on the back. Rick loved his Harley so much that he had the Harley-Davidson insignia tattooed on his left upper arm.

Fully aware of the young couple's predicament, Damon said, "You're welcome to share our pop-up camper."

Rick noticed that the camper didn't have a real tag, just a cardboard one that read "Lost License."

Their blue and white Cadillac needed some repairs, Damon told him, and he hadn't been able to fix it yet.

"Maybe you can help me, Ricky. You know, to repay my kindness."

"What's wrong with it?" Rick asked, accepting the Busch offered to him.

"It sometimes won't start. I think it's the timing chain. You know anything about that?"

"I'll take a look in the morning."

Rick didn't know shit about a timing chain, but he figured, if he said he did, they'd get to hang around a little longer. Damon had an ice chest full of beer, and he was willing to share it.

In the end, Damon went to the campground office and used a pay phone to call a mechanic, who came and fixed it. Damon didn't like having to pay someone to fix his car, and he took it out on the rest of them.

Rick soon learned that his new friend was a first-rate Southern asshole, always issuing orders to Loralei.

"Get me a beer. Don't cook them hot dogs till they're black, will you, bitch?"

Rick was on the receiving end of those orders as well. He didn't like it, but there wasn't much he could do about it. Damon was providing the money and the food, the beer and the weed. Rick wondered where Damon got his money, but he didn't ask since he only had five bucks in his billfold.

Rick didn't like camping. It was hot as hell, and the mosquitoes were terrible. But the carnival wasn't set to open for another week, and it was the only job he'd been able to find. He'd stayed with his sister in Topeka and looked for a job there, even filled out an application to work at McDonald's. Desperate, he felt like a huge screw-up. He'd married before he got his GED from Topeka West High School, divorced, remarried, and divorced again. He had a kid, a little girl, who lived with his parents outside of Fort Lauderdale.

He'd felt lucky when he got the job with the carnival at the Kansas State Fair and met Chantina, a pretty little thing with dirty-blonde hair and eyes that sparkled when she looked at him. Rick liked the ladies, and they liked him. That's what always got him in trouble. He'd operated an escort service that was successful in Fort Lauderdale, but he'd had to close it after the second divorce. His wife had gone into the business on her own. They'd owned a few with names like "Southern Comfort" or "Mad'mo'zell," but most of the profit was spent on cocaine.

So there he was on that fateful day—the 10th of September, 1980—in a shitty motel in Fort Smith, Arkansas. Tied in with a guy who promised a big score from a little jewelry store across the Arkansas River. Damon bragged that he had already cased the store, and it would be a piece of cake.

Damon and his wife had gone into the store on the previous Wednesday, pretending to be shopping for a wedding set. The owner was a short, crippled guy, who walked with two hand crutches. His wife was friendly and showed them several rings. They'd chitchatted, mostly about the hot weather.

Loralei had raved over a big diamond engagement ring and asked, "Honey, can we afford such a beautiful ring?"

Damon had answered in the sweetest Southern drawl he could muster, "Darling, I'd beg, borrow, or steal anything you wanted."

The crippled guy's wife was wearing earrings and a ring that Loralei liked as well. The couple stayed in there a long time, so long that Damon sensed the wife was getting suspicious because a young girl who'd been in the back came out to stand next to the wife, who turned out to be her mother. Both the women clerks kept their eyes on them, so they left the store. They didn't leave the shopping center, though, but sat in their old Cadillac, watching what time the store closed, where the owners parked their cars, and what make they drove. Turned out the couple drove a Mercury, and the daughter drove a green Suzuki jeep.

They hadn't stayed long because they knew their old Caddy and their camper would be conspicuous. They'd come back again. But first they had to find the campground they'd seen on a tourist map of Arkansas. It was up in Rogers on Beaver Lake.

When they'd arrived at Horseshoe Bend, it had been close to nightfall, and good fortune led them to Rick and Chantina.

Damon and his wife drove down again to Van Buren to case the jewelry store on the following Saturday. That time they just looked around, claiming they were killing time until a movie started. A different woman was working then, and she drove a blue '76 Camaro.

On their way back to Rogers and the campground, Damon decided he'd ask Rick if he was interested in making some money. Although Rick had already told him he'd never been in trouble with the law, he had an anxious air about him. Rick complained about not finding a job and how he'd always had luck with the ladies, but he'd like to have some luck with getting some money too.

Damon needed another man to help him, and if Rick agreed, they would go back to Van Buren again on Monday, spend the night at a cheap motel, and let Rick check out the jewelry store to get the lay of the land, so to speak.

Rick had agreed without hesitation, and on the 8th of September, they'd said their goodbyes to the girls and driven south, found the cheap motel that suited their purposes, and set their plans in motion. First, they went to a bar and had some beers. They then drove over to Van Buren, and Rick visited the jewelry store while Damon walked around the shopping center. They'd met up again at Safeway, the store across a busy highway where they'd parked the motorcycle.

Damon was leaning against the motorcycle, puffing on a cigar.

"Well, how'd you make out?"

Rick sat down on the concrete that was shaded by a large oak.

"A daughter of the crippled guy waited on me. I flirted with her and asked as many questions as I could without making her suspicious, but she acted a little funny. She was a good-looking brunette with long hair and real brown eyes, and her sister, a cute little thing if I've ever seen one, came out of the back room and stood with her till I left."

"But you saw everything?"

"Oh, yeah. There are four horseshoe-type cases. Two on the right, and two on the left. The watches are on the back right, and the diamonds are across the store from them. The counter and cash register are in front of the back door that leads to a room where the crippled guy usually stays."

They then rode up two or three blocks, scouting for an apartment complex that would fit in with their plans. They found one: the Sleepy Hollow Apartments.

The next day, Tuesday, they rode back to Cloverleaf Plaza. On that trip, Damon wore a brown lady's wig under his helmet. In the parking lot, Rick saw a blonde, and he hollered to her: "Hey, good-looking, want to go get a beer?"

The girl waved back and came over to where they were standing. She had a cast on her left leg, which she said she'd broken in a motorcycle accident. She told them her name was Pat Etier and that she lived in Graphic, a little community close by. She agreed to take Damon in her truck to buy some beer over in Fort Smith. Rick followed, and then they all went back to the Terry Motel.

The men had told her they were passing hot checks and just working their way toward Oklahoma and then Texas. Damon took off his wig, revealing his dyed blond hair, and Pat thought it was the funniest thing she'd ever seen.

Damon and Pat flirted with each other, and before long Pat invited Damon home with her for the night.

"I've got to be back in the morning by eight," he'd said after lighting a cigar and puffing on it to get it going. "That's eight on Wednesday morning." And then he tossed a ten to Rick.

Rick waved goodbye and headed to The Branding Iron, a bar he and Damon had visited on their first day in Fort Smith. He liked the atmosphere there.

At precisely 8:00 the next morning, Damon opened the motel door with his key.

"Honey, I'm home," he called to Rick, who woke up at his arrival.

Damon lit a cigar and smiled real big. "I feel pretty relaxed. Me and that woman screwed our brains out. It's good to get some strange every once in a while."

Rick agreed and lit up a cigarette before heading to the bathroom. For the moment, Rick thought, Chantina was enough for him.

Damon opened the briefcase he'd carried with him when the two of them rode on Ricky's motorcycle down from their campground. Damon hummed a country song—"popular in Georgia," he said—and laid out at the foot of his bed a woman's brown wig, rope, a .22 revolver, a .38 pistol, a homemade silencer, and two orange nylon duffle bags.

"Get some washrags from the bathroom," Damon ordered. "They make good gags. You know, to keep people from screaming."

CHAPTER THREE

Suzanne Ware, the youngest of the Staton daughters, sat in front of a fan that was set up on the kitchen cabinet. It was already hot that Wednesday morning on the 10th of September as she laid her diary on the kitchen table. She had started writing in her brand-new journal exactly a year ago. She read to herself how she'd opened:

Keeping a journal will be a new experience for me. I want to try it, partly for myself and partly for my family in the future. I have enjoyed reading my grandmother's and my aunt's diaries, so maybe someday someone will enjoy mine. I do plan to give more than facts. I'll try to give my thoughts and feelings.

Instead of writing in her diary, she thought about the coming suppertime her family would spend together at her sister Karen's new house. Suzanne had seen the house first and told her sister about it. They both agreed it had possibilities. They would be within walking distance from each other, and Karen, handy with a paintbrush and a hammer, wasn't afraid to tackle any project. She had even figured out how she could cook a spaghetti supper for her family without a kitchen stove.

Another sister, Elaine, and her little boy, Ben, lived close by and were coming too, and she looked forward to playing with her adorable nephew, who would be two in December. Janet, the sister just a year younger than Karen, lived in Paris, Texas, so she couldn't be there. Suzanne missed her. It would be sad without her when they all sat down to dinner that night.

Suzanne wanted to get in a little studying before she showered and dressed for work at the jewelry store. Her clothes for the day, a navy flowered dress and ankle-strapped wedgies, were laid out on the bed she'd made up after she'd kissed her husband, Tom, goodbye.

He was a musician, and he and his band were playing that night at the Camelot Hotel in Tulsa, Oklahoma. He was picked up by his friend, Jimmy Atchison, another guitar player, and they had some last-minute arrangements to make before leaving around four that afternoon. The other members were leaving earlier with the equipment.

Sometimes she went with him and listened to him play. He sang, wrote songs, and played the guitar, and she'd fallen in love with him in the ninth grade. They had married on January 26th, 1976, when they were both nineteen.

She lifted her long brown hair off her neck and stood in front of the fan. Even her gold cross necklace she always wore felt hot around her neck.

Suzanne walked into the bedroom and let her hair fall back down her back. Hair like hers was the style of the '70s and '80s, but she wondered how she'd look with short hair. She had a pretty face and dark-brown eyes, like her parents, and she'd been told she had a pretty figure, even if she did only weigh a little over one hundred pounds.

While her husband dreamed of making it big in the music business, she longed to become a vet, and with that ambitious dream, she'd just begun college courses at Westark Community College in Fort Smith. She planned her class hours around her full-time job at the jewelry store, purposely not scheduling classes on Wednesdays because it was Karen's day off. It was a good day to get to work with her dad. She was the only daughter who had shown a talent in watch repair, so she worked side by side with him at a long table in the back room.

Karen pretty much ran the front where the glass display cases were. She was good at arranging gift items and decorating for the different seasons. Karen also ordered the merchandise and patiently and expertly waited on customers. Their mother, always on call, helped when needed, which was most of the time.

Kenneth Staton had a policy that there would always be two people in the store, especially at closing time. The threat of robbery was always there, of course, and he'd cautioned his family that, if that awful thing were to ever happen, they were to cooperate—that nothing was worth losing their lives. He refused to keep a gun for protection because he said he could never shoot someone.

Suzanne loved her parents. She and her sisters were close, and they all pitched in as a team to help in the family business. Since their father never complained about his inability to do what other fathers might, they didn't either. The sisters were aware of their mom's devotion and hard work, especially when she had worked the night shift at Dixie Cup for four years to pay the bills while their dad was in the hospital for surgery or rehabilitation in Memphis or Hot Springs.

Suzanne felt lucky. She was surrounded by the love of her family, her husband, and her new family, the Wares.

Her only complaint on that Wednesday, September 10th, was the heat. The awful, terrible heat. It was just too hot to think about writing in her diary. She'd do it later that night, after she got home from Karen's.

* * * * * *

Ruth Staton moved a little slower than usual that Wednesday morning. She had fixed bacon, scrambled eggs, and made toast for breakfast, and then poured herself an unusual second cup of coffee. Her husband had driven their car to work, so she didn't have to get dressed as early as usual. She lingered over the coffee and read last week's *The Press Argus*, the local weekly where they often advertised. She was pleased that Karen had taken over that aspect of the business. Karen was artistic. She filled the display cases in a pleasing way and decorated the store windows with seasonal flair. She knew the inventory, maybe even better than her dad.

Ruth's mom, Juanita Greenfield, lived in the Cavanaugh section of Fort Smith, and she'd insisted Ruth keep her car while she visited another daughter in Oklahoma City. Ruth liked having a second car, even for just a little while. Her mother was really good to her. She and Kenneth had moved in with her family after they had married at a too-young age. Ruth had dreams of becoming a nurse, and Kenneth had told her he'd always wait on her. But they were in love and couldn't wait, so they married when she was seventeen and he twenty.

"Ruthie," he'd told her, "I know my rheumatoid arthritis will probably make me a cripple someday if they don't find a cure. Are you sure you know what you're getting into?"

Ruthie had kissed him and said she didn't care. But she did care. Not for herself, but for her husband. She was used to bad things happening. Her family was poor, like many others during the depression, and she'd almost died of diphtheria when she was a baby. And when she was fourteen, while running from a boy who was trying to kiss her, she'd fallen off a forty-foot cliff, injuring her right leg so badly the doctor had said, "We'll try to save her life first before we even think about trying to save the leg."

She'd spent four months in the hospital before she could go home, minus her first pair of blue jeans that had to be cut off after her fall.

But Ruth Staton was strong, and she knew her husband was a good man. A proud man. When he'd showed her an ad in a magazine advertising a watch repair correspondence class, she encouraged him to take it. They didn't know how they'd get the seventy-five dollar fee together, but they knew the Good Lord would help them. And He did. In fact,

Ruth and Kenneth Staton credited God with everything good that ever came their way. They still belonged to Central Presbyterian Church in Fort Smith—one of the churches they'd attended while they lived in Fort Smith—and continued attending there now that they lived in Van Buren on Azure Street.

She and Kenneth had been married thirty years, and on their twenty-fifth wedding anniversary, she had given him a beautiful diamond wedding band. She also had two pretty rings of her own—a showy cluster diamond ring and a ruby and diamond ring—both befitting the wife of a jewelry store owner.

Ruth looked at her watch and decided her loafing hour was over. Suzanne would be working with her that day since Wednesday was Karen's day off, and she knew they had over twenty-some-odd watches and jewelry items waiting to be repaired and made right again. She would be at the store all day until almost closing, when she would leave to return her mother's car to her since she was getting home from Oklahoma City that night. She hoped Kenneth and Suzanne could get a lot accomplished. Ruth felt good about business. It was always slow during the summer, but lately it had really picked up. Yes, she thought, things were looking good for the Statons.

CHAPTER FOUR

At Horseshoe Bend, Chantina and Loralei had walked to the camp showers early that Wednesday morning. They wanted to beat the other campers and get the hot water while it lasted. Chantina liked being close to the lake. It was pretty, almost like being close to an ocean, which she'd never seen before so it didn't really matter if it was a lake or an ocean. In Topeka, Kansas, it was flat and dry, and the only water she'd ever swum in was at the city pool, and she'd only done that a few times. It cost money, and she didn't have any.

She missed Ricky and his Harley. She'd always had a penchant for guys who rode Harleys. And Ricky was good-looking—a couple of inches shy of six feet with dark eyes and dark, wavy hair. They were in the throes of first love or passion or whatever you wanted to call it. She just wished he wasn't so poor, but she seemed to always fall in love with the poor guys. The good-looking poor guys who rode Harleys.

Loralei never let her out of sight. It was as if she thought Chantina would leave.

Think about it, Chantina considered telling her. *Where am I going to go, and how will I get to where I'm supposed to be going to?*

Although she and Loralei were about the same age, she felt Damon's wife was way more worldly than she was. Loralei drank too much, and she bragged in her thick Southern accent that she had drug connections in Cobb County, Georgia, and on Stewart Avenue in Atlanta.

Chantina wasn't a Goody Two-Shoes. After all, she was a carnie, but she felt like there was a time and place for getting shit-faced drunk. Loralei started her day that way. And she liked men and wasn't ashamed of showing off her cute little body, which was about a size four. In that hot weather, Loralei wore cut-off shorts that showed off her butt and halter tops that showed off her tits. Chantina caught Ricky looking at them once, and she told him, if she saw him do it again, she'd tell Damon. Ricky had denied it, but she knew better.

When Chantina got working again, she was going to dye her hair the color of Loralei's, a pretty dark brown. She was flat broke now, and there was nothing left for her to do but get along. She sure would be glad when Ricky got back. They'd been gone for three days now, doing something that nobody wanted to talk about, but Ricky told her he'd soon have some cash in his billfold, and she could buy anything she wanted.

"Be patient," he'd told her.

And so she was. As patient as she could be with a crazy alcoholic following her around.

Loralei was born in Alabama. She'd lived off and on with her maternal grandmother, Sue Brooks, the only parent figure she'd ever known. She smoked her first marijuana cigarette when she was thirteen and then graduated to Quaaludes, cocaine, morphine, and Dilaudid. Her drug of choice was alcohol, though, and she'd spent time off and on in juvenile detention centers before graduating to county jails. She was pretty and could talk her way out of trouble some of the time. Damon wasn't really her husband. In fact, her real name wasn't Loralei, and his real name wasn't Damon. They'd gotten in a little trouble at a campground in Tyrone, Georgia, so they changed their names. Sometimes it was hard to remember.

The guys would be back that night. And she couldn't wait to see what Damon would bring her.

CHAPTER FIVE

Cloverleaf Plaza was a nice shopping center that had been developed in the late 1960s by a long-time Van Buren citizen, C.C. Gunn. His nickname was Pistol, for obvious reasons. His son, Johnson, was well known as a handsome athlete of the early '50s, who drove a red convertible and kept a Bible in his back pocket. His younger sisters, Judy and Jane, were beautiful and exceptional in scholastics and popularity. Anything Pistol Gunn touched turned to gold—even his children. And in the Gunn tradition of excellence, the shopping center was thriving.

In that hot September of 1980, the shopping center consisted of a drug store, a dress shop, a Hunt's Department Store, a Walmart, a movie rental place, a sporting goods store, an optical shop, an Otasco store, a laundromat, a radio station, and a small bank. And beyond the parking spaces, across the busy 64-71 highway—four lanes with congested turn lanes—sat Safeway, a large grocery store with a small deli and bakery. And next to it, by some elm trees, another bank.

It was in that Safeway parking lot that Ricky Anderson parked his motorcycle at the side of the store. He and Damon Peterson had visited a pawn shop in Fort Smith earlier in the day and pawned a ring of

Damon's for forty-five dollars, which they needed to tide them over until the pay day that would come around six o'clock.

After looking around to see if anyone had seemed to notice them, they hung their helmets over the handlebars. They then went inside the front door to a cold drink machine, and Ricky bought a can of Dr. Pepper and Damon got a root beer. Each looked at the clock above the door as they walked out.

5:45.

Back in the parking lot, Ricky took a long drink and commented on the heat coming off the asphalt while Damon opened the saddlebag on the back of the motorcycle and pulled out a briefcase. He looked around, but he didn't see anyone close by. He handed a .38 revolver wrapped in a Walmart sack to Ricky and stuck a .22 pistol in his jeans and pulled his shirt down over it.

With the briefcase under his left arm and the root beer in his right hand, he jerked his head toward the Cloverleaf Shopping Center across the street.

"Let's do it," he said.

CHAPTER SIX

Ruth Staton grabbed her purse and said a quick goodbye to her husband and daughter around 5:30 p.m. on Wednesday, the 10th of September. She saw the look on Suzanne's face that said *Mother, you're leaving early?*

"Remember? I've got to take Nanny's car home to her."

"Oh, yeah. I forgot. See you later at Karen's."

On the way out, Ruth spoke to a teenage girl who was looking at rings through the glass case.

"I'm sorry I can't wait on you. Suzy will be with you in just a minute."

"Oh, that's okay, Mrs. Staton. I'm just killing time while my mom's in Walmart. I'm looking at birthstone rings. My eighteenth birthday is October fifth."

"Oh, Brenda, I didn't recognize you at first. Your hair has gotten really long. Well, you tell your mom I said hello."

On the drive to her mother's home on the south side of Fort Smith, Ruth thought about Brenda's mother, who had just started a new job as a checker for Safeway in Fort Smith. Her husband was home, out of work, because he'd fallen off a ladder while he was nailing down some loose shingles. He'd broken his right arm and right leg and would be off work for a long time.

In earlier years of her marriage, Ruth had once worked as a checker for Safeway, so she knew how hard that job was. The pay was okay, but she was pretty sure there wouldn't be enough money for a ring for Brenda. If Kenneth found out that Brenda wanted the ring so badly, he'd probably help her family make some payment plan. He was much more tender-hearted than she was.

The traffic on Interstate 540 was bad, so she decided she'd better pay closer attention to the road. She passed the exits for Rogers Avenue, Greenwood Avenue, Zero Street, Highway 71, and then, at Exit 13, she headed down busy Jenny Lind to Cavanaugh Road.

She parked her mom's car in the garage and went inside her house, where she found the plants watered and the blinds opened. Her mom's next-door neighbor had been there to get her house in order. The house was warm, but Ruth didn't dare turn the air down. Her mother was very particular.

Ruth walked through the house, making sure everything was as it should be, and then she walked into the living room and stood at the big picture window. From that view, she could watch for Kenneth, who would be arriving soon to pick her up so they could get back to Karen's house for supper.

Karen had purchased an older home she was remodeling, and the kitchen stove had been removed. Since Wednesday was her day off, she had invited her entire family for supper, even though she had to use a crock pot to fix the spaghetti.

Ruth was proud of Karen, as well as her other daughters. They had never caused their parents any trouble, as many teenage girls are prone to do, and now they had grown up to be responsible adults. Two of them had made her a grandmother.

Her watch read 6:20. Kenneth should be there any minute now, and she went over all the things she must do after the spaghetti supper. They were leaving early on Thursday morning to go up to Fairfield Bay for the weekend. They had signed up for a promotional tour the newly developed vacation resort was offering to folks willing to listen to an hour's sale pitch in exchange for a stay in a condo on Greer's Ferry Lake.

Six thirty arrived. She telephoned the store, but there was no answer. Six forty came. No Kenneth.

Ruth walked outside and looked down the street for any sign of him. It was too hot to stand on the driveway pavement for long, so she went back inside. Her dress was wet around her waist, and her forehead was dripping with little beads of sweat. Where was Kenneth? Perhaps he'd stopped to fill up the car. She realized her heart was pounding, and she felt slightly nauseous.

Where is Kenneth?

* * * * * *

Suzanne sighed, thankful she'd finished with Mrs. Newton's watch before closing time. It was hard not to finish a job and have to start all over the next day. At least that's what it felt like to her. Her daddy had been working on watches so long that he was able to just pick up and finish, even if a day or two had gone by.

She liked Mrs. Newton, and she was glad they had a mainspring on hand. She placed the gold Bulova in the "to call box" inside one of the safes. They were both opened because her daddy had started his closing down chores and was emptying some of the cases already.

She reached across the work bench and turned off the radio. She was glad her dad hadn't minded that she brought it from home. She loved music, and KISR was her favorite station. Music made her think of Tom, and she hoped he was already in Tulsa with the guys, setting up at the Camelot.

Suzanne stood up and pushed her chair under the table. She'd worn a dress to work, and she was anxious to get home and change into shorts. Karen was cooking spaghetti for everybody, and Suzanne was hungry.

She joined her daddy in the front of the store.

"Well, Daddy, I finished the Bulova."

The front door opened. A young guy about her age smiled. She noticed he had really white teeth, but his jeans were dirty and looked as if he'd worn them way past wash day. He looked familiar to her, and then she remembered he'd been in the store earlier. Karen had waited on him.

The young guy set a Dr. Pepper can down on the top of the glass ring case.

"I was in here before, looking for a ring for my girlfriend."

Her dad nodded hello and walked behind the ring counter.

"Hot enough for you?" her daddy asked. "A nice rain would be welcomed."

The young guy didn't answer but kept his head down and didn't even look up.

How rude, she thought. She was overly protective of her daddy, and she didn't like for people to ignore him.

Another man came inside and he, too, was carrying a canned drink, only his was a root beer. Lots of people carried something to drink in this heat, but they didn't usually bring it into the stores. *Rude,* she thought once more.

Suzanne walked over to help the second guy, who looked like he was wearing a brown wig. *What's up with that?* she thought. He was tall and sort of soft looking, and a pungent scent of cigar smoke and sweat clung to his body. He smiled real big. A zap of alarm ran across her shoulders, her stomach, her legs.

What are two men like this doing here right at closing time?

She looked to her daddy, but she saw he was writing out a ticket. She guessed the young guy with the white teeth had bought something. But then she saw the man reach behind his back and pull out a pistol.

"This is a robbery," he said—not loudly, but in an everyday tone of voice.

Her daddy dropped the pen and turned around, his face a pale gray.

And at that moment, the guy with the wig took a gun out of his Walmart sack. Something long was attached to the barrel.

29

"Put your hands up, little girl. We're going to that there back room."

Her daddy was clutching the handles of his crutches so tightly that she could see his arms quiver, but he smiled at her and said, "Just do what they say, Suzanne."

She wasn't sure her legs would support her body. She felt weak and nauseous. Once again, she looked to her daddy—the man who'd been her champion, her hero, her everything all her life. She was afraid he couldn't help her now.

"Do what they say," he repeated. "Everything will be okay."

After they walked to the back room, the guy with the wig told them to take off their jewelry. He seemed to be the boss.

Suzanne took off her wedding ring, clutching it in her fist until she had to hand it over to the young guy.

Her daddy gave the guy with the wig his diamond wedding band, a ring he'd been given by her mother for their twenty-fifth wedding anniversary.

The guy with the wig held out his hand, palm up.

"Your wallet too, old man."

Normally, her daddy didn't carry cash, but she knew he had cashed a check on his lunch hour. He and her mama were going on a little break. When she thought of her mama, she began to cry.

Her daddy said, "Now, now, Suzy. We'll give these men what they want, and then they'll leave. Right, fellas?"

"On your belly. Tie 'em up," the guy with the wig said.

The young guy pulled their arms behind their backs and tied their hands together with a thick, scratchy rope. Then he looped it around their ankles, pulled it around their heads, and cinched it tightly across their mouths that had first been sealed with what felt like washcloths. He didn't say a word to them.

But the guy with the wig assured them they weren't going to get hurt.

"We're just going to tie you up so we'll have a head start when we leave here. Just do what we say, and I assure you nobody will be hurt. That sound like a deal?"

The men went back to the front, and she could hear them taking the jewelry out of the cases. Maybe her daddy was right. If they just cooperated and did what the men said, it would all be over quickly. She tried to remain calm, but it was hard to breathe.

When the men returned to the back room and the young guy asked if her car keys were in her purse, she could only nod her head yes.

"Where's the purse?"

She glanced at the top of one safe, where she routinely kept her purse.

The young guy had already laid his gun on the counter while he was tying them up, but the guy with the wig was now holding his long gun just inches from their noses.

They will kill us, Suzanne realized. She knew they would.

She thought about Tom and hoped he knew how much she loved him. They had been arguing lately, but that didn't mean anything. All couples have fights. She thought about her dog, Pearl, and hoped she would be okay without her. Her mama would miss her, and so would her sisters. And little Ben? She wouldn't get to see him grow up.

Oh, Daddy, what are these men going to do to us? Will it be quick?

Her daddy's glasses sat askew on his forehead, and she could tell he was in a terrific amount of pain. His crutches lay on the vinyl floor at his feet.

Oh, Daddy, I love you so much.

It was then that she saw the guy with the wig place his gun against her daddy's right temple and pull the trigger. Blood spurted out into a big, wide circle under his sweet, sweet face.

She knew she was next, but thankfully she didn't have more than a second to ponder how it would feel to have a bullet in her brain. She fainted at the precise moment the guy with the wig pulled the trigger.

The young guy yelled, "Why'd you do that?"

"No witnesses," the guy with the wig said.

He shot each of his victims in the head one more time to make sure they were dead.

CHAPTER SEVEN

At Karen's house, her kitchen table was beautifully prepared with the blue carnation patterned dishes her mother had given her. It was the same set her daddy and she and her sisters had bought for their mom for Christmas when they were little. They bought it at Sears, and their mom had loved it.

Years later, after her mom and dad had moved into the house on Azure in Van Buren, and she had gotten another set of China, her mom passed the original dishes down to Karen because she now had a home of her own.

"You can set the table and invite us all over for dinner," her mom had said.

Karen looked down at her kitchen floor, which was covered with orange and yellow linoleum patched together with silver masking tape. The countertops were covered with drab, gray linoleum. When she'd bought the house, she knew it would require lots of work, but she had seen the potential. It had the original wood floors, and the ornately carved front door had stained glass window panes that had been painted over. That door had once been elegant, she thought, and she would one day make her whole house elegant again.

But for now, her table looked pretty, and that reminded her of going to a really fun Christmas Sunday school party at her teacher's house when she was nine or ten years old and her family attended Temple Baptist Church in Fort Smith. The teacher was very poor, and she'd lived in a small house set close to a highway. The teacher had served cookies and hot chocolate in Mason jars, way before it became popular to do so. Karen had realized then, at that early age, that it didn't really matter where you ate or how it was served. It was the loving spirit of an event and the people who gathered there that were important. That night, she was having her family over for dinner to celebrate her ownership of her home, and it didn't matter what the floor looked like.

Elaine and Ben had been at Karen's since 6:00 that evening, and like any toddler, he was getting into things. He had been in Mother's Day Out at the Central Presbyterian Church in Fort Smith and missed his nap. Elaine was trying to help, but mainly she just kept Ben out of mischief. They expected Suzanne any minute. She was walking over once she'd changed into shorts after work. Because of the heat, all the girls wore shorts. Karen had pulled her hair up in a barrette to get her long hair off her neck.

"Suzanne should have been here by now, don't you think?" Karen said, looking at her watch.

She had the French bread buttered and waiting in the toaster oven, and the salad was in the refrigerator. The spaghetti was on low in the Crock-Pot.

"You know," Elaine said, "I dropped by the store earlier, and Suzy was about to leave for lunch. She asked me if I wanted anything, but I told her I had other errands to make. I left before she returned. I bet they just had some late customers."

"Yeah, I guess. I hope that's what it is."

* * * * * *

Ruth Staton paced back and forth across her mother's living room, and each time she heard a car coming down the street, she raced to the front window.

33

No Kenneth.

At 6:45, she decided to call Karen from the phone on the kitchen wall, even though she didn't want to needlessly alarm the girls.

"Is your dad there?"

"No, Mom, he isn't."

"Is Suzanne?"

"No, but Elaine and Ben have driven over there to see if she's home yet. Wait a minute, Mom. I just heard a car pull up."

After a moment, Karen returned to the phone.

"Mom, Suzy wasn't home. We'll drive down to the store."

At that moment, Ruth and Karen and Elaine had each reached the conclusion that their family had been visited by something terribly wrong.

"Mom, we'll call you."

As Ruth waited for the phone call, she fretted and fretted, and she thought she could actually hear the beating of her heart.

Kenneth would never have not called me if he was just running late.

She dialed the store's number, but it was busy. After four or five minutes, she called the store again. It was still busy. She called Karen's house again and got no answer.

All the busy signals and no answers didn't make sense, so she decided to call the police. Nervously, she opened the phone book to look for the number, but then she realized she knew what it was so she dialed it.

When she heard a man's voice answer, she said, "There's something wrong at Staton's. Would you send someone out to check?"

"Are you Mrs. Staton?"

"Yes."

"Can you go there?"

"Yes." And then she hung up.

She stood by the phone a minute, thinking she might faint. Her face was hot, and the rest of her body felt cold. She didn't know if she would be capable of driving back to Van Buren. Then she thought about calling someone to come and get her, but that would take time. Precious time. She went out into the garage, opened the door, and climbed into her mother's car. It wasn't far to I-540, so she began the thirteen-mile trip that would be the longest of her life.

Off to her right, she briefly noticed a golden field covered with dried corn stalks and cracked dry soil. She'd always hated September, when the whole world seemed hot and the color of ripe persimmons she used to step on when she was a little girl. They'd squished between her toes, and wasps would buzz around the fruit, threatening to sting her bare feet. Like in that field, everything started to dry up and die in September.

For years after, whenever Ruth drove on the interstate and passed that field, she would remember (although she never really ever forgot) that hot September day when her life was changed forever.

Staton's: Only Van Buren Jeweler

Staton's Jewelry is the only jewelry store in Van Buren and the owners of the business have an attractive shop in Cloverleaf Plaza which will cater to all your jewelry needs.

The business is owned and operated by the Kenneth Statons, who opened the business in Van Buren in 1960 in a store downtown. They opened another store in the shopping center located on Alma Hwy. three years ago and continued running the store downtown. In recent weeks they have been holding a close-out sale in the downtown store and should be moved completely to the Plaza this week.

The Cloverleaf Plaza store is a spacious place situated in 2,250 square feet between Hunts Department Store and Gennill's dress shop. It is filled with display tables and along the walls are shelves also used for display.

The business handles a general line of jewelry merchandise; giftware of crystal, pewter and silver and also watches. It also offers a repair department which will repair any kind of jewelry and watches brought in. The only thing they do not repair,

Staton said, is clocks.

Along with the selling of jewelry merchandise and its repair, the Statons have on hand wedding books from which wedding napkins and other accessories can be ordered through the shop.

The Statons, who live in Fort Smith, have all pitched in to help with the operation of the business. Staton is in charge of all repair and his

wife, Ruth, works in the shop doing anything which has to be done, Staton said.

His daughter, Karen, age 25, is the assistant manager, and does a little of everything from waiting on customers to placing advertising and buying and ordering merchandise.

Two other daughters, Suzanne and Elaine, have both worked in the store, and

Staton said, only one of his four daughters have not worked there.

One part-time employee, Peggy Parks of Van Buren, works as a sales clerk.

Staton's is open from 9:30 a.m. until 6 p.m. Monday through Saturday. The business will stay open until 9 p.m. during December to facilitate cusomers with shopping.

Kenneth Staton and his daughter, Karen, work steadily to operate the family-owned business, Staton's Jewelry.

KAREN AND KENNETH IN NEWSPAPER ARTICLE

CHAPTER EIGHT

Elaine drove her car to Cloverleaf Shopping Center. Because they were in such a hurry, Ben sat in Karen's lap. When they pulled into the parking lot, they saw that Suzanne's jeep was gone, but their daddy's Mercury was still there. They parked and walked to the front of the store and saw that the lights were still on. The front door looked like it was locked. Karen didn't have her keys with her, so they walked into Hunt's Department Store next door.

"Have you all seen our dad and sister?" Karen asked.

Buster Fowler, the night manager, saw the anguished look on the girls' faces.

"No, what's wrong?"

Elaine held Ben in her arms, and even he had a puzzled look on his face.

"The lights are still on, but the door is locked. We don't know where they are."

Mr. Fowler shook his head in disbelief.

"Let's go look."

They walked next door and stood at the glass doors. Upon careful examination, Mr. Fowler saw that the door was shut, but the top and bottom were not locked. He pulled on the door, and it opened.

Once they were inside, Karen took one look at the empty glass cases and yelled, "We've been robbed!"

Mr. Fowler followed Elaine to the back of the store, but Ben and Karen remained in the front.

Elaine immediately saw her dad and Suzy on their stomachs on the floor with their ankles and hands tied. There were gags in their mouths, and blood was pooled on the floor. She saw the holes in their heads and thought they had been hit with something like a baseball bat. Mr. Fowler immediately picked up the phone that sat on the long work table and called the police.

Elaine yelled as loud as she could. They had been hit so hard, they could just be unconscious and unable to hear her. She wanted them to know she was there with them.

"Daddy, wake up!" she shouted. "Suzy, wake up!"

Elaine knew her daddy hadn't been able to lie on his stomach for years, and she intimately recognized how uncomfortable he must be.

"Oh, Daddy. Oh, Daddy."

She was the only one who really understood the horrible and often constant pain caused by rheumatoid arthritis. It was a condition that she alone shared with her sweet daddy.

Elaine knew her daddy and sister were really hurt bad. They may have even been dead, but she had to help them in some way. She grabbed a pair of scissors and tried to cut the ropes that bound them.

She then rushed into the front of the store where Karen and Ben were.

She still held the scissors in her bloody hands.

"Why did they have to hit them so hard!" she yelled.

And then Elaine and Karen were both screaming.

Mr. Fowler and some ladies who worked at Hunt's had come inside and were tending to Ben. One of the ladies took the scissors away and wiped off Elaine's hands.

Karen went to the phone at the front desk to call an ambulance, but just as she reached for the phone, the police arrived. She dropped the phone, and it dangled off the hook, creating a busy signal for her mother, who would shortly be frantically calling the store.

The policemen told the women to please leave the store and let them do their job.

"You can wait outside."

Elaine held Ben in her arms, trying to soothe him by telling him not to be scared.

Karen refused to cry because a crowd of people were already gathering, and she didn't want anyone to see her crying. It also seemed like, if she didn't cry, then everything would be all right.

But Elaine had seen the blood matted in her little sister's long brown hair and the blood from her daddy's head slowing spreading along the vinyl floor.

Karen had not seen the bodies, so she was more hopeful.

"When the ambulance comes, they'll take them to the hospital, and everything will be okay."

But when help arrived, the attendants went inside the store and came out without their daddy and sister.

"Go back! Don't come out without them!" Karen screamed.

A policeman Karen didn't recognize walked up to them and said, "We're going to put you young ladies in a police car where you'll be safe."

KENNETH AND ELAINE

CHAPTER NINE

When Ruth arrived at the shopping center, cars and trucks and police cars were parked here and there in front of the store. People were milling about, and in the crowd Ruth recognized several friends. Three ambulances were parked side by side. She stopped her car in a traffic lane and got out. Through the crowd, she walked directly to the store. Just outside the store, she asked a woman driver of an ambulance, "Why are there three ambulances?"

The woman looked as if she was confused and didn't know how to answer the question.

"One broke down, and we had to call another."

Men with cameras were taking pictures behind yellow tape that had already been strung up around the store. Ruth saw a white car with the Channel 5 logo on the doors. In minutes, other television stations would be sending their cars as well.

Ruth continued walking to the jewelry store, but when she got to the front sidewalk, a man stopped her.

"You can't go in there."

"But my family is there," Ruth said.

"Ma'am, ma'am." And then, very firmly, he said, "*You do not want to go in there.*"

Ruth turned her head and saw a policeman ushering Elaine and Karen into a police car. She walked toward them, and when the policeman saw her, he said, "Get in. We're taking you all to the hospital."

At that time, Ruth felt some hope. Maybe Kenneth and Suzanne were at the hospital. Maybe everything would be all right.

But when they reached Crawford County Hospital, which was only ten minutes away, the police car pulled into the emergency entrance.

A plump nurse with a kind face came out to the car. She stuck her head through an opened window.

"Why don't you come inside?"

Ruth asked, "Why? Is my husband here? Is my daughter?"

The nurse smiled. "No, I'm so sorry. We thought you might want to come inside, in case you needed some treatment to help you cope."

Ruth was afraid they would give her a shot that would knock her out, and she wanted to be alert if her husband or daughter needed her. With as much determination as she could muster, she said, "I don't want anything like a shot or anything else."

Following their mother's lead, her daughters said they didn't want anything either.

The police officer drove them back to the shopping center parking lot. In the middle of the crowd, Ruth saw a car she recognized with her friend Tressie Marchbanks inside. She was a dear woman, who had taught all four Staton girls in elementary school. She had even home tutored Elaine for four years when Elaine wasn't able to attend school because she, too, had developed rheumatoid arthritis.

When the policeman stopped the car, Tressie Marchbanks walked over to them. She put her arms around Ruth and her two daughters and little Ben.

"Get in our car. We'll take you home."

Ruth climbed into the front seat behind Tressie, whose husband sat behind the wheel. Tears flowed down his red cheeks, and he tapped the steering wheel with his fist in short, quick pats.

Inside the safety of the car, Ruth finally admitted, "I guess they are both dead."

Tressie put her arm around Ruth and whispered, "Yes, dear."

Ruth then turned to look at her daughters and grandson in the backseat. The daughters nodded their heads yes and then looked out the window. Ben had already fallen asleep in his mother's lap.

No words were spoken on the drive home. Tressie suspected they were all in shock and were incapable of voicing their pain. She also knew that the Statons were a stoic family, used to hardships and debilitating illness, and were not prone to let others know their true feelings.

Tressie's husband, Odie, trying hard to hide his anger at what had happened to the finest family he'd ever known, drove slowly and carefully to the Staton's home on Azure Hills Drive.

When Ruth and her two daughters walked into their home, it was there that their nightmare really began and would never, ever leave. Years would pass, and Ruth and her daughters would have to find their own way to live with the trauma of the cruel and heartless reality of the deaths of Kenneth Staton and Suzanne Ware.

If Ruth hadn't left early, she would have died along with Kenneth and Suzanne. If the crime hadn't happened on Karen's day off, she would have been there instead of Suzanne. It was a series of what-ifs that would haunt them for a very long time.

Ruth Staton tried to reach Elaine's husband at his workplace at a plant in Sallisaw, Oklahoma, where he was head of the maintenance department. She was stalled several times by men who answered the phone but didn't know how to locate Bill. Finally, she got him on the phone and told him the dreadful truth of what had happened. Bill was upset to hear the news about his father-in-law and Suzy, but he was more concerned for his wife, Elaine, and their little boy. He rushed to the Staton home on Azure Hills where the family was gathering.

Tom Ware, Suzanne's husband, was playing in a band at the Camelot Hotel in Tulsa. His parents rushed to Tulsa from Rogers (where they lived) to tell him what had happened.

In Paris, Texas, the bewildered Riggs couple and their two children began the three-hour trip to Van Buren. Janet tried not to cry in front of Jon and Sara, but it was impossible. Her heart was broken, and she was angry that a good man, who had worked hard all his life under the worst of handicaps, and her sweet little sister had been brutally murdered by evil men or women or both. She wanted to know the details, but when she would ask Tommy if he knew how they died, she would cover her ears and say, "No, no, don't tell me. I don't want to know."

Officials from the State Medical Examiner's Office remove the bodies
... for transport to Little Rock at about 11 p.m. Wednesday

REMOVING BODIES ON SEPTEMBER 10, 1980

CHAPTER TEN

With the keys from Suzanne's purse, Damon and Rick had jumped into the green Suzuki jeep and sped across Highway 64-71 to the Safeway parking lot. Damon jerked off his brown wig and threw it into one of the orange bags of jewelry.

Rick was swallowing back bile. If he'd been alone, he would have vomited on the floor of the car.

"What the hell was that all about, Damon? Shit! I don't know what's going to happen next! I didn't sign up for this crap. Those people are dead, Damon!"

"Shut the fuck up, you pussy!" Damon yelled back at Rick. "I told you, 'no witnesses.'"

They didn't see Billy Ray Miller headed home from his job at Planter's Peanuts, but Miller noticed that they were driving a little fast into a grocery store parking lot, so he watched as the jeep stopped and a man climbed out and walked toward a parked motorcycle. Miller watched as the jeep left, with the motorcycle following close behind. Miller thought nothing more about the incident until he finished his grocery shopping and looked across the street to see police cars parked in front of Staton's Jewelry Store.

Linda Godwin, an employee of Oklahoma Gas and Electric Company, worked in a small kiosk at the shopping center. She had noticed two men walking briskly across the shopping center around 5:45. One had long hair and the other had scraggly hair. She had wondered to herself where they were going in such a hurry. When she later heard about the robbery, she figured out where they were headed.

* * * * * *

Rick had slammed the door and jumped out at Safeway. He thought briefly of just getting on his Harley and heading back to Kansas. But Chantina was back at the camp, along with what little clothes he owned, and he still only had five bucks in his pocket.

He followed the jeep to the Sleepy Hollow apartment complex three or four blocks away. Damon parked the jeep and threw the keys into a drainage curb beside the parking lot. They then drove across the bridge to the Terry Motel and gathered their belongings.

"Why'd the hell you have to kill 'em?" Rick asked again.

He felt sick to his stomach and realized he wasn't cut out for that kind of life. He felt scared, more scared than he'd ever been in his twenty-three, almost twenty-four years on earth. His years of being drug to the Seventh Day Adventist church by his parents came flooding back to him. What would his mother say? His dad?

Damon jerked Rick's arm and turned to face him.

"No witnesses, you goddam fool! I keep telling you!" he shouted. And then, as if fearful someone had heard him through the motel's thin walls, he lowered his voice to a whisper. "No witnesses."

Rick was more frightened by Damon's whispered voice than his screaming voice.

"Okay," he said. "I thought it was going to be a simple robbery, that's all."

Damon laughed. "A simple robbery? Hell, man, there's no such thing as a simple robbery."

"Yeah, well, you didn't say anyone was going to get shot?"

"I gave you a gun, and you carried it. What did you expect, you pussy?"

"I thought that was just for show," Rick said, his voice breaking. "You said if you carry a gun then nobody gives you a hard time." His eyes were filling with tears, but he didn't want to cry in front of Damon. "Just to show we meant business. Or something."

Damon placed his hands on either side of Rick's face and pressed hard.

"Listen, you are in deep shit. As deep as I am. So you keep your mouth shut. Don't tell Chantina. Don't tell nobody, you hear? We're going to leave this shithole and get up to Beaver Lake. We're going to act calm, drive the speed limit, and get up there by dark."

Rick pulled Damon's hands off his face. He was angry, and there was no chance in hell he was going to cry. He spat out the words: "I get it."

In a matter of minutes, they were out the door of room 18. As Rick started the motorcycle, he waited for Damon to go inside the office to pay the bill to the Iranian man who stood behind the desk. Rick watched Damon peel off some bills from *his billfold*, knowing they came from the *crippled guy's billfold*. He heard Damon say in a loud Southern drawl, "You have a nice day, you hear?"

A thought raced through Rick's head, over and over. It was an old saying of his father's and probably his father's father as well: *In for a dime, in for a dollar.*

※ ※ ※ ※ ※ ※

When Ricky and Damon roared into their campsite around 9:00 at night, Chantina and Loralei were sitting around talking to two men who had walked over and struck up a conversation with the girls.

Damon threw his leg over the side, stepped off the Harley, and rubbed his hips. He took off his black helmet, reached into his shirt pocket for a cigar, and lit it with great aplomb.

They all chit-chatted about fishing and how hot and humid it was for a minute or two before the men realized they should quickly make their exit.

Damon pulled Loralei tight against him and patted her rear.

"We made a killing, baby."

Chantina hugged Rick and whispered, "Thank God you're back. I was going crazy with that woman."

"Shh," Ricky said, whispering in her ear. "Keep your damn mouth shut."

Chantina lowered her gaze and kicked at the dirt with her bare foot. Rick had never talked to her like that.

"What'd I do wrong?" she whispered. "I missed you a lot. I didn't mean nothing by what I said."

"Just cool it," Rick said. "Quit asking questions."

Damon yelled, "Hot damn, girls! Get in the trailer."

The trailer bed was cramped with all four in there at the same time. Everyone except Damon sat down while he dumped two orange nylon bags on the floor. Diamond rings, watches, necklaces, bracelets, gold chains, and cash lay in a jumbled pile. The price tags were still on most of the pieces, and some items were still in their boxes.

Loralei feverously racked her fingers through the men's signet rings and other obvious rings for men and pushed them aside. Then she pored through the ladies' jewelry.

"Where's the earrings I wanted and the ring?"

"The older lady wasn't working, so I couldn't get them. Quit your bitching."

Damon and Rick then sorted the jewelry and watches according to what they were worth. Some of the men's rings were priced at close to $2,000. The cheapest one was $200. Everyone tried on various rings and bracelets and held their hands up to the light to see the sparkling diamonds. Damon knew the ones he wanted, but he kept his mouth shut about that for now.

The girls were allowed to choose some less expensive pieces, like bracelets or necklaces. Chantina surmised quickly that Rick and Damon had robbed a jewelry store, but she didn't know where, and she didn't know how, and she didn't want to know. Some small part of her conscience knew stealing was wrong, but damn, those gold chains were beautiful, and she'd never owned anything pretty before in her life.

Loralei put her hand on Rick's shoulder and said with a smirk, "So how you like working with Damon?"

Rick didn't answer, but shrugged his shoulders.

Maybe he smiled, maybe not. All he could think about was a crippled man and a young girl lying face down, with their wrists and ankles tied together with ropes, the ropes he had tied around them, and their mouths gagged with strips of washrags that came from the Terry Motel.

And blood. Lots and lots of blood. Blood from two bullets fired at close range into the head of the man and two bullets into the head of the pretty girl with long, light-brown hair.

His thoughts were jolted from that bloody past to the terrifying present by Daman laughing loudly and talking to nobody in particular.

"Down on your knees, dog," he said, as if he were reciting a line from a play or a bloody event that had recently occurred.

Everyone laughed, even Chantina, but she had no idea what was so funny.

Rick and Chantina spent the night in their sleeping bags, away from the camper where Damon and Loralei slept. Chantina tried to lure Ricky out of his bad mood with her usual way of getting a man to be nice to her, but it didn't work. Rick tried to perform but couldn't, and that made him act even more hateful. They slept on the nylon bags with their backs resting against each other, while those in the camper were having a good time.

CHAPTER ELEVEN

The next morning, Rick and Chantina rode on the motorcycle into Rogers to a pancake house while Loralei and Damon followed in the old Caddy, leaving the camper at the campsite in Horseshoe Bend. They were hungry since none of them had eaten anything the night before. Damon had bought a newspaper out of a rack by the front door before he went inside, so he read while he ate and didn't chit-chat with anyone at the table. Loralei ran her mouth, as usual, while Rick and Chantina didn't say much of anything.

After breakfast, the men dropped the girls at a discount store while they went to a used car lot.

"We got to get rid of the Caddy," Damon said.

"You worried about the timing chain?" Rick asked. "I thought it was fixed."

"Hell, no. We don't need a car that someone may have seen at that shopping center."

The Economy Car Lot in Rogers, Arkansas, was the kind of lot that would trade for a car with no questions asked, so they made a deal for a dark-green, four-door Plymouth from salesman Michael Jeffcoat, who didn't have to try too hard to convince them that it was the car for them.

When they picked up the girls later, Loralei told Damon it was the ugli-est car she'd ever seen.

Damon laughed. "I didn't buy this car for its looks, baby. I bought it so nobody will give us a second glance."

They then drove back to Horseshoe Bend and broke camp. They built a small fire in the pit to burn the boxes and price tags that came with the jewelry, as well as the beer cans and garbage that had accumulated in the trash barrel. Damon didn't want any trace of them left behind.

"Just for safety's sake," he said.

Damon hooked the pop-up camper to the Plymouth, and Rick fol-lowed on his Harley to Fayetteville, a short distance away. At 1790 Birch Avenue, where Fayetteville Self Storage was located, they parked. Da-mon went inside and waited on the proprietor, who came from a back room. He spoke pleasantly and gave Damon a ballpoint pen that adver-tised the address and phone number. Damon didn't converse with the nice man but let him know that he was in a hurry by tapping his fingers on the counter. He signed a receipt, rented a ten-by-twenty-foot storage compartment, and told Rick to back the trailer into the small space. He then parked his Harley beside it and hung their two black helmets over the handlebars. With a heavy heart of having to leave his pride and joy, his dark-blue 1978 Sportster, Ricky pulled the door shut and locked it. The stolen merchandise was safely hidden in the briefcase in the trunk of the Plymouth.

With that accomplished, they filled up the tank at an Esso Station, and by 5:00 the afternoon of the 11th, they left town to drive straight through to Atlanta.

Left behind were the good folks of Van Buren. It didn't seem to mat-ter if they personally knew the Statons or not. They knew what the newspaper said and what they saw on television, and it was all incred-ibly sad. There was no other way to put it.

CHAPTER TWELVE

By the time Ruth and her daughters reached the Staton home at 205 Azure Hills, friends and some family members were already arriving. A Channel 5 newsman, who had happened by and seen the crowd of people and police cars gathering in Cloverleaf Plaza, reported to the newsroom of the robbery and murders, and it was broadcast immediately. The names of the victims were even announced, regardless of the policy of waiting until all family members had been informed.

Grady Staton, one of Kenneth's older brothers, was sitting in his living room recliner in front of the television when he heard the news. He later told his sister-in-law that he was so shocked that he thought he might die from the heart condition that had forced him to retire early. He began formulating the story in his mind that would later be printed in *The Press Argus* called "Side by Side."

Fay Watts arrived at the Staton home with her twin daughters, Linelle and Michelle, who, at the ages of fifteen, were offered as babysitters for little Ben. They put him in a highchair and fed him supper, which was long overdue. Later, after his daddy had done his best to console Elaine, Bill took Ben home with him and left his wife with her mother and sisters.

The L-shaped living room, dining room, and kitchen were filling up with people, including the wife of C.C. "Pistol" Gunn, who said her husband was so upset he'd become physically ill and couldn't come in person.

A guest bedroom was designated the smoking room, and the smokers stayed in there. Elaine, after not smoking for three years, joined her sisters and lit a cigarette—and would continue to smoke until she became pregnant with her second son, Alexander.

Outside in the front yard, knots of people stood around. Many of the women cried openly and clutched neighbors' hands. The men, with hands in their pockets, murmured their disbelief that something as horrible and tragic as the murder could happen in their little town, especially to the most respectable family in their midst. Some men expressed anger and used their most vile vocabulary of words to express their hatred of the lowlife who committed the crime.

Evelyn Hess, a friend and neighbor from up the street, took Ruth's address book to the master bedroom and began dialing the phone numbers of those listed in Ruth's sprawling handwriting. With each conversation, gasps were shared and then tears.

Even thirty-five years later, random acts of sympathy, such as flowers, cards, and food, were recollected by the family. Karen remembered a small gift of a stained glass Bible verse dropped off that night by a casual friend and high school classmate, Lindey Cotner, who felt like he had to do something.

Phyllis Kincy, a vivacious young mother, had only worked part-time at Staton's for a week before the robbery. The police asked her to come down to look at the store to see if she saw anything unusual. She did not. Even after that experience, she still wanted to work at the store, so when she made her condolence call at the Staton home, she told Ruth that, if they reopened, she wanted to continue working there.

Ruth's cousin, Warren MacLellan, and his wife, Wanda, came to offer support. With Ruth's permission, they decided they could best help by parking in front of the jewelry store to hold vigil over the bodies until they were taken by the coroner to Little Rock for autopsies. Ruth knew they were the perfect ones to represent the family since Warren was no stranger to frightening experiences. He had been an aircraft carrier pilot, who had crashed in the Pacific in World War II, surviving not once but twice in situations that should have killed him. He and Wanda were made of strong stuff.

Kenneth's youngest sister, Rita Gray, arrived with her husband, Tom. A friend of theirs had heard about the robbery on a police scanner and called the Gray residence with the news that Kenneth had been killed, along with one of the daughters. They had immediately rushed from their home in Fort Smith, not knowing which one of the daughters was killed.

All the way to Van Buren, Rita had thought about her young days of growing up during the Great Depression. How she'd played marbles and cars with Kent, who was just three years older than she. In order to have a playmate, she had to play boy games, instead of dolls and paper dolls that she would have preferred. And how when they were older, they'd played Rook, and that Kent was very competitive and didn't like to lose.

She remembered how the family had worked in the fields picking cotton, and how Kent didn't ever pick the most, but his was the cleanest, without leaves or stalks in his sack of cotton. And how he loved fishing and hunting, but after the arthritis got him, he could no longer do what he loved the most.

She also remembered the sacrifices Ruth had made because of Kent's confinement to a wheelchair. She was the breadwinner for many years, and after their marriage, they had moved in with Ruth's family. Her mother helped Ruth care for him because he was in constant pain.

"Oh, how far they've come," she said aloud to her husband. "And now this. Who would hurt Kent?"

When Rita and Tom walked into the house, they saw Karen standing in the kitchen. That was the way they discovered that it was little Suzy who had been shot and killed.

Ruth Staton was standing in her laundry room in front of the dryer when Rita found her. They hugged each other, and Rita said, "How could anyone do this to Kenneth?"

Within the hour, the lawmen, who faced the huge challenge of solving the crime, sat at the kitchen table—refusing offered cups of coffee, anxious to get as much information from the family as possible. They knew how frightened the remaining Statons were.

"Whoever killed your dad and sis are long gone. They would want to get out of Crawford County as soon as they could," Sheriff Ball explained.

Karen remembered that a tanned young man with longish brown hair had been in the store on Monday, shopping for a wedding ring.

"He stayed a long time," she recalled. "And his teeth were very white against his skin. He laughed a lot. It was a nervous laugh, and he said he guessed he should spend more on this second wife than he did on the first wife. He stayed so long that Suzanne came out from the back and stood at the counter with me. I remember saying, 'If he's for real, that will be a good sale.'"

Listening closely was the police chief, Virgil Goff; the assistant chief, Wayne Hicks; the Crawford County Sheriff, Trellon Ball; and the Arkansas State Police investigators, Doug Stephens and Don Taylor. The prosecuting attorney, Ron Fields, stopped by as well, offering condolences and assurances that everything would be done quickly and efficiently to find and arrest the murderers. Crimes of that magnitude rarely happened around there, and the local law enforcers welcomed the help from the better trained and more experienced state investigators. Those men would prove to be the heroes in the Staton Jewelry Store robbery and murders by finding the men responsible in only sixteen days.

CHAPTER THIRTEEN

Tom Ware, Suzanne's husband, and his band, *Bajer*, were about forty-five minutes into their set in the ballroom of the Camelot Hotel in Tulsa when an employee of the hotel told Ware he'd received an emergency phone call from his brother, Steve, in Fort Smith. As soon as they finished playing "Little Jeannie" by Elton John, Tom left the stage.

Tom went out to the lobby and called collect to his brother. His sister-in-law, Melanie, answered the phone.

"What's going on, Mel?"

"It's Suzanne! Some guys went into the jewelry store and robbed it, and they shot Suzy and her dad."

"How bad are they hurt?"

Melanie was crying so hard she couldn't answer.

Finally, after a long minute so Tom could get his breath, he asked, "Is she dead?"

"Yes, yes!" Melanie sobbed for a long time until she could get the words out. "Your mom and dad are driving over from Rogers to pick you up."

When the guys in the band took a break, they found Tom in the lobby, and he told them what had happened. They were all upset as well, but they decided to finish their gig without him. At that point, there wasn't much they could do to help him.

Tom went outside and stood in the parking lot for close to an hour, waiting on his parents to arrive. He smoked one cigarette after another while he paced across the asphalt and cried.

Inside, the band played on.

When his parents, Albert and Stella Ware, arrived, they headed to Van Buren by way of the Muskogee Turnpike. The three of them knew nothing of the details, so all they could do was speculate. Tom kept insisting that his dad drive faster.

"Dad, speed up. God won't let anything else bad happen to us tonight."

They arrived at the Staton house around 10:30 p.m. Karen and Elaine were there with Ruth, and they tried as best they could to tell the Ware family what had happened. Everyone was sobbing, and Tom felt especially sad for Elaine because she was the one who had found his wife and his father-in-law, a man he admired greatly because of his strength and fortitude. He also remembered that Kenneth Staton said he wouldn't keep a gun in the store because he would never be able to shoot another person.

Even though Tom's parents offered to take him home to his house and spend the night with him, he elected to stay at the house on Azure. He felt some degree of comfort by staying among his wife's family, and eventually he found a spot where he could lie down and sleep.

The next day, he was taken to the State Police Headquarters and questioned. He found out later that he was, at first, considered a suspect simply because he was a close family member and that's the way police worked. But, of course, he had been in Tulsa, following his dream.

CHAPTER FOURTEEN

Like Tom Ware, the next morning found Ruth, Elaine, and Karen at the State Police Headquarters on Kelly Highway in Fort Smith. Each was asked questions in a separate room with just the investigator.

"We must ask if you know anything about a rumor we've heard from a prison informer who tells us that Kenneth Staton dealt in stolen diamonds and, in fact, kept a lot of money and diamonds in his safe."

The three Staton women were still in shock, but they knew, for sure, that their dad/husband did not deal in stolen diamonds, and to suggest such a thing was highly insulting.

And over the years, whenever that particular question the police had asked them about their father crossed their minds, each wondered: *Where did that information come from? Who said that?*

* * * * * *

On that same morning after, the regulars at the Cottage Café didn't have much of an appetite. The coffee cups were filled and refilled, but no eggs and bacon were ordered, no biscuits and gravy. At least not for a while.

"Bad news travels fast," one customer said, looking around at the men who were usually involved in laughter or mild arguments over politics or sports—the usual banal conversations of men in early morning cafes throughout Arkansas.

His friend, Louis, only three days shy of eighty, agreed. He spat tobacco juice into a white plastic cup he kept in the bib of his overalls and said, "I hope they find them sons-of-bitches and string 'em up quick. I don't want Mrs. Ruth worried they're coming back to get her and them other daughters."

＊ ＊ ＊ ＊ ＊ ＊

Don Taylor, an investigator with the Arkansas State Police, was once again at the Staton Jewelry Store the morning after the crime. He was busy taking photographs, bagging a root beer and a Dr. Pepper can left behind by the robbers, tagging a sales slip dated 9-10-80 in the handwriting of Kenneth Staton, and examining the rope used to tie the victims. He was called to the phone to talk to an attorney for a young woman who said she might have information about the robbery.

As he listened to what the attorney said, a wide smile crossed his face, and he took another drag from his cigarette.

"Call the sheriff, and let him take it from there. I'll call Ron Fields and let him know."

Taylor was a seasoned investigator with the state police, and he had a pretty good sense of what was good information and what was not.

"Boys, I'm out of here. I'll be at the sheriff's office."

Taylor was tall and lean with thick gray hair. He hadn't slept much the night before at his Fort Smith home, but he felt like a million bucks after he'd heard from the attorney. He drove the five or six minutes to the Crawford County Courthouse and rushed to the sheriff's office.

＊ ＊ ＊ ＊ ＊ ＊

Down the street and almost at the river's edge of the Arkansas, Sheriff Trellon Ball sat at his desk in his office in the Crawford County Court-house. His feet were propped up on the green felt cover protecting the finish of his desktop, marked by other sheriff's boots that had rested there while their owners tried to figure something out. Sheriff Ball was deep in thought and high on caffeine.

Not too long before, he'd received a call from an attorney who told him he had talked to Don Taylor and that Taylor had told him to call the sheriff.

"And?"

"I've got a client who knows something about the Staton robbery."

"Well, bring him in."

"It's a her, not a him."

"Well, whoever it is, come on down, or do you want me to come to your office."

"We'll be there at eleven."

Trellon looked at his watch for the fiftieth time. It was almost 11:00, and he wished they'd just come on. He wished he'd been able to get a little shuteye the night before. He wished for a plate of his wife Ruby's good-old scrambled eggs and hot biscuits with butter and honey. He wished for a clean shirt. He wished the Staton family members hadn't been murdered. He wished he could get the smell of blood out of his head.

His phone rang, and he jumped. He sat straight up in the chair and put his feet on the floor.

"Sheriff Ball," he answered.

It was Ron Fields, the prosecuting attorney, and the sheriff knew he'd been up all night also.

"I understand you had a call this morning that might be helpful. I'm coming over right now."

"Yes, sir," he said. "See you shortly."

Ball dropped the phone into its cradle.

This must be something big, he thought, *for Ron to come to my office.*

Trellon Ball was a God-fearing man who attended the Baptist Church in Alma. He didn't drink, and he seldom swore. But today, that morning, that most tragic of tragic mornings, he said aloud, "Damn, I hope we catch those evil bastards. And something tells me we're going to do it. And soon."

"Talking to yourself?" Don Taylor asked. He'd walked in just in time to hear the sheriff.

"Yeah, I'm psyching myself up."

They heard a slight knock on the door, and they looked around to see the familiar face of a young lawyer who hung around the courthouse with a pocketful of business cards. With him was a woman with brown, shoulder-length hair who wore a dingy-looking cast on her lower right leg. In her right hand was a cigarette.

The sheriff stood up and motioned to the two maple, straight-back chairs that sat in front of his desk.

"Have a seat."

"This is Pat Etier," the lawyer said. "She is pretty darn sure she has some information about the Staton robbery."

"Yes, ma'am," the sheriff said. He picked up a pencil and began to write on a yellow legal tablet that lay on his desk. "How do you say your name again? And spell it?"

"E T I E R. Like a tear from your eye."

"Okay. You can start your story, if you will."

"I met these two men this week. This past Tuesday in the Walmart parking lot here in Van Buren. The young one hollered to me and said something like, 'Hey, come have a beer with us.' They were on a motorcycle, and we got to talking. The one that owned the motorcycle— a Harley—was named Rick. He was in his early twenties, I'd say. His friend's name was Damon, and he had died blond hair, but he was wearing a woman's brown wig. Both had on black helmets. When Damon took off his helmet, his wig came off. We got to talking and . . ."

The sheriff was busy scribbling notes and looked up to see Ron Fields enter the room. Fields was a good-looking guy, a decorated Vietnam veteran, and smart as a whip. He was dressed in a navy suit and white shirt.

"Sir, this is Pat Etier, and I think you know her attorney."

Ron Fields nodded to both, pulled up a stool, and sat next to the sheriff.

"Sorry for the interruption. I'll catch up. Keep talking."

"Well, anyway, I followed them to their motel over in Fort Smith, and then we went in my truck to get two six-packs of beer. We went back to the motel, the Terry Motel on Midland, and drank it. The man called Damon and I, well, we sort of hit it off, and I gave him a picture of me with directions on how to get to my house. But he ended up riding with me back to my house in Graphic."

"Graphic? That's close to Mountainburg?" the sheriff asked. "And what age is this Damon fellow?"

The girl nodded her head yes and said, "Damon told me he was thirty-six. I have a little boy, and we picked him up at my babysitter's house before we got to mine. We ate supper and sat around and talked. And then, well, you know."

Ron Fields stood up, removed his coat jacket, and hung it over the back of a chair. He placed his hands under each arm, obviously sorting through the information he was hearing.

"How long did this man stay at your house?"

"That's just it," she said. "He made me promise to get him back that next morning by eight o'clock. He said he had some important business to take care of. And he always carried this briefcase with him."

"What business did he say he was in?" Fields asked.

"They both said they were passing checks."

"And did you get him back on time?"

"Yeah, but you know what I'm thinking now? He asked me that morning at my house if I had a pistol, and that he'd like to teach my little boy how to shoot a gun. He said, since my boy didn't have a daddy around, he'd like to teach him some manly things. I told him I didn't."

Her eyes filled with tears, and her lips quivered.

"I think, if I'd had a gun, he'd have killed my boy and me."

"You've done a good thing, coming in here," the sheriff said.

"When I saw on the news last night about that robbery in Cloverleaf, and that's where I met those two guys, my heart stopped, and I thought I might have a heart attack. I grabbed my boy tight and hugged him so hard I scared him."

Ron Fields walked across the room to the windows and looked out on the courthouse yard. The leaves from the tall elms had already begun to fall because of the hot summer with little rain. The grass was only green around the edges of the fountain, and the pink petunias planted in beds were leggy with few blooms. It was just too damn hot.

"Ma'am," Ron Fields said, "you're a brave woman for coming in. We're going to get a sketch artist in here to see if you can give him some good descriptions of these men. Did you see any tattoos on them?"

"The young one had a Harley-Davidson emblem on his left shoulder. He showed it to me. He was real proud of it."

"And the other one. The man who spent the night with you?"

"He didn't have one." She lowered her head, obviously embarrassed to be talking to three law-enforcement men, the kind of men she preferred *not* to talk to. "He was a little paunchy, with a double chin. He did not have a tattoo. I saw him naked, and he didn't have a single one. Not anywhere."

Sheriff Ball blushed. Ron Fields did not. The lawyer smiled. Don Taylor rushed out the door.

Even before he turned on the air conditioner in his car, Taylor was reading his notes on what he'd just heard and formulating his plans. First, he'd cross the river to the Terry Motel on Midland Avenue and see what he could find out there about the two men who rode a dark-blue or black motorcycle.

* * * * * *

Heat waves shimmered across the pavement at the entrance to the Terry Motel. In the noonday sun, the motel looked even more woebegone and run-down than it did at night. A cloud of despair and hopelessness seemed parked in front of each cabin.

Taylor stopped his car by the office door and walked in. He introduced himself to the dark-skinned man behind the desk, whose nametag read Patel.

"I need to look at your registration books for the nights of . . . let's say, September eighth and ninth."

Patel opened the book to those dates and moved it across the counter.

"I'm looking for two guys who rode a motorcycle," Taylor said.

Patel walked around the counter and stood next to Taylor.

"I remember them, yes," he said, pointing to a name: *Damon Peterson.*

Taylor could smell the man's curried breath.

"And is there a license plate number?"

"393656 Florida Harley-Davidson motorcycle. A party of two."

CHAPTER FIFTEEN

When Ruth, Karen, and Elaine returned from the State Police Head-quarters, they saw cars parked up and down the street. Thankfully, there were no cars in the driveway, so they were able to park Ruth's mother's car in the garage. They would make the car exchange later after the Staton's Mercury was fetched from the Cloverleaf parking lot. Elaine's husband had already picked up her car, and a friend of his had driven the grandmother's car home to Ruth.

Inside, the kitchen table was covered with plates of sandwiches, cakes, pies, casseroles, chips, two meat and cheese trays, and a variety of soft drinks. Paper plates and napkins were on the kitchen counter, along with plastic cutlery. And in the living room and dining room, bouquets of carnations, mums, yellow roses, blooming azalea plants, and African violets dotted every flat surface in the room. Some flowers had to be moved into the bedrooms because there was simply no more room in the living areas.

The sight of the flowers made Ruth teary, and she felt comforted by the kindnesses shown her and her daughters. She wanted to read every card, but she felt almost nauseous from lack of sleep and despair.

Her friend, Evelyn Hess, was there again—answering the knocks on the door, accepting food brought or flowers sent. She tried to get Ruth to go back to her bedroom and lie down, but Ruth said she knew she couldn't sleep.

"I'm afraid to close my eyes," she said.

Karen and Elaine retreated into the smoking room, the aroma of the flowers making them feel light-headed. They wondered how they would ever get over this senseless tragedy that had happened to their family.

Ruth knew she needed to hold it together because the funeral home and the minister of the Central Presbyterian Church in Fort Smith had already called about making arrangements.

"Oh, me," Ruth lamented to her cousin Warren MacLellan, who had arrived while the women were at the police station. "I never thought I'd be the one planning Suzanne's funeral."

* * * * * *

On September 13th, the closed-casket services for Kenneth Paul Staton and Suzanne Staton Ware were held at the Central Presbyterian Church in Fort Smith—a red-brick church with white columns and a tall white steeple on Roger's Avenue, one of the busiest streets in the city. It was a beautiful church and looked like one from a picture postcard.

Without fanfare or broadcast, the entire funeral expenses were borne by the members of that church. The minister, George Gilmour, was a tall, slender man in his late forties with two adult children. He delivered a painfully difficult message to those who had gathered for the 11:00 a.m. service. He had prayed for God's help in finding the right words, the comforting words, that would help the crowd gathered in the sanctuary. Tall windows with wooden shutters kept the hot September sun out, but dappled sunlight still fell on the shoulders of mourners who sat in the cushioned pews.

"We are here," Reverend Gilmour began, "because we have experienced a part of life which is most painful. Death is an inevitability which comes to everyone of us. It always comes as a thief in the night . . . .

"Of course we are angry at the apparent irrationality of the act which took Ken and Suzanne from our midst. The only answer that even begins to make sense is described by the theological word *sin* . . . ."

The service was concluded with a beautiful hymn that some of the congregation knew from memory: "A Mighty Fortress is Our God." And if not all the words were able to be sung, the tune was hummed through gently falling tears.

The burial was held at Woodlawn Cemetery on State Line Road, close to the boundaries between Arkansas and Oklahoma. Because of the intense heat, the minister announced that the cemetery service would be short. Tombstones not yet placed would eventually be laid side by side—exactly the way in which father and daughter had sat at the long work table repairing watches, and exactly like father and daughter were found in death. Side by side.

The following day, Janet's husband, Tommy Riggs, made preparations for young son Jon and him to return to Paris, Texas. Jon needed to get back to school, and he needed to return to work. Tommy knew there was something he must do before he left, and he threw back his shoulders, took a deep breath, and told himself to be a man.

He and a friend of Karen's went down on Sunday afternoon to clean the jewelry store's back room of the blood from Kenneth and Suzanne's injuries. It was a difficult task, and no conversation took place. One spot was left, a spot that could not be removed, no matter how much bleach was poured on or how hard the men rubbed their mops. Finally, they gave up, and they returned to the family, who was still staying at Azure Hills.

The three Staton daughters were sitting around the dining table, watching the Staton grandchildren play in the backyard. A welcome cloudy, late-afternoon breeze had caused the mothers to relent and let the children burn up some energy. Little Ben loved his older cousins, and they were both kind to him and included him in their made-up games.

When the men walked in, their faces were ghostly white, and they didn't speak. Tommy looked at his wife, Janet, and shook his head from right to left, as if to say, *Don't ask me about it.*

The spot of blood remained, long after Staton's Jewelry Store re-opened for business. The family asked their insurance company if they would pay to have the floor replaced, and the answer was no. And there the spot remained, a constant reminder of what had happened at closing time on September 10th, 1980.

CHAPTER SIXTEEN

The two couples in the green Plymouth drove the 720 miles from Rogers, Arkansas, to Atlanta, Georgia, in less than eleven hours. They stopped in Memphis for gas and a bathroom break and continued driving straight through. It was there that they would fence the stolen jewelry.

The trip was anything but pleasant, with drunken bickering going on between Damon and Loralei while Chantina and Rick barely talked. Once, while Rick was driving, Damon got so angry with Loralei that he choked her and held a knife to her throat. They had all taken uppers, and their nerves were shot.

When the two couples checked in at the La Quinta in Atlanta, they breathed a sigh of relief at getting away from Arkansas. Rick still had not told Chantina what happened at the jewelry store, and she didn't press the issue. All she knew was that she and Rick were pretty much stuck with Damon and his wife.

Damon was anxious to get the jewelry sold, so he called a few of his friends who had contacts. He was directed to a man who was currently a patient at Grady Memorial Hospital. Damon visited him there in the ICU, and the exchange of some items was made.

The next exchange, one not nearly as bizarre, was done at a man's home. All in all, the pair received around $15,000. Damon got sixty percent, and Rick got forty.

After spending two nights at the La Quinta, they checked into a more luxurious hotel, the Omni. There they stayed and lived it up with good food, good whiskey, and lots and lots of beer. They walked through the new CNN Center that had opened in 1976, but seldom were the men completely at ease.

Rick was afraid of Damon, so he was always on guard. He quieted that fear by drinking from the minute he woke up and throughout the day.

Chantina felt lost, and even though she had joined the carnival to see something besides Topeka, she wished she was there now.

Damon Peterson smoked high-dollar cigars and strutted around with his dyed blond hair and his brown mustache that didn't match his hair, trying to play the role of a Southern aristocrat.

Loralei stayed high or drunk most of the time.

On their last night in Atlanta, they moved to another hotel, a cheaper one, realizing that their money was going fast. At the Landmark Inn, while out to dinner, their room was broken into and the two guns—the .22 and the .38—were stolen, as well as their clothes and the jewelry they had kept.

"Goddammit," Damon said. "Can you believe this shit?"

Loralei laughed. She laughed at everything when she was high or drunk or both.

"It's ironic, isn't it? Robbers robbed by robbers."

Damon drew back his fist, as if to hit her.

"It is kind of funny," he said.

And then he laughed too. Just before he slapped her hard across her face with the hand that wore Kenneth Staton's wedding ring.

Rick wanted to grab Damon, tell him to cool it, but instead, he reminded Damon that they needed to leave Atlanta.

"Whoever stole our stuff might come back, and we don't want to be here."

The next morning, they checked out and drove to a car lot where Damon bought a cream-colored 1976 Cutlass. They left the ugly green car at the Atlanta Airport and headed for Jacksonville, Florida, where they could buy more guns, as many as they wanted.

After shopping for more clothes and purchasing several guns and silencers from a guy Damon knew, they rented two motel rooms on Jacksonville Beach and drank beer and swam in the Atlantic.

On the second day there, Damon pulled Rick aside from the girls and said, "You need to get rid of Chantina. She knows too much. I'll kill her for you if you'll return the favor."

Rick was especially sweet to Chantina that night. He told her she was a wonderful girl, and that she shouldn't be hanging out with him. He was afraid something would happen, and she'd get arrested if he ever got arrested.

"I want you to go back to Topeka in the morning. I'll tell Damon we need to use the car, and I'll take you to the bus station." He folded together two one-hundred-dollar bills and placed them in the pocket of her jean shorts. "This will get you home safe with a little left over."

Chantina cried because she didn't want to leave Rick, but she was glad to get away from Damon and Loralei. They were scary, and they had both told her many times that, if she ever told about the jewelry store robbery, they would hunt her down or have someone else do it for them.

Somebody was always watching her. She couldn't do anything without Loralei by her side. Once, when she called home, she tried to have some privacy by taking the phone into the bathroom, but Loralei followed her. She couldn't even write a note on a postcard unless Damon approved what she wrote.

CHAPTER SEVENTEEN

On Monday morning, the 15th of September, Karen woke with a start. She was still staying at her mom's house because her mom was afraid to be by herself. She would continue to live there until after Christmas.

Karen had been grieving over her father's and little sister's death and had thought of nothing else. But that morning she realized, as she heard her mother in the kitchen, that she and her mother depended completely on the jewelry store for their livelihood. If they closed the store, how would they live? They had to have an income. The store still had some merchandise, and there was a lease on the store, and home mortgages and electric bills and water bills to be paid, and groceries to be bought. She wanted to stay in bed with the sheet pulled over her head, but she had to get up. She simply had to function again. They owed it to her daddy.

For the past ten years, Karen had worked full-time in the store. She had learned buying, advertising, engraving, and bookkeeping from her father. She was proud of the Staton's Jewelry Store. Proud of her father, who had worked hard to build the business. She vowed, much like Scarlett O'Hara in *Gone with the Wind*, that she was not going to throw away everything because she was too sad and scared to open the doors again.

Karen pulled on the shorts she'd worn the day before and grabbed a clean cotton shirt out of the laundry basket on the floor by her bed. She walked into the bathroom and came out more determined than ever.

"Mom," she said as she poured a cup of coffee, "I want to talk to you about something."

Ruth patted her daughter on her shoulder. "Let's sit down."

Bottles of Coke, Pepsi, and Dr. Pepper still sat on the kitchen counter, and just that morning, a neighbor from across the street had brought over a loaf of banana bread. Two loaves of fancy bakery bread, pumpernickel and rye, had yet to be opened, and the refrigerator was so full of casseroles that Ruth had sent home some with Wanda MacLellan and Evelyn Hess.

"We'll never eat all this food," Ruth said, looking around her kitchen that was usually immaculately clean and straight. Her eyes were puffy and red around the rims, and she looked as if she'd aged ten years. Her hair needed shampooing, but she had no energy for anything more than a quick shower. What she wished she could do was crawl in the bathtub and stay in warm water all day.

Karen said, "Mom, we have to reopen the store."

"Oh, I can't. I can't go back there. No. No."

Karen almost cried, and she thought she might not be able to stop. But she got control of herself. She called it detaching, and she would detach for a long time. It was the only way she could get through it.

"Mom, it's our livelihood. We need the store, and I don't want to throw away everything Daddy worked for."

Ruth spread her hands out on the table and studied them. She had strong hands with long fingers, and she realized how much they looked like her mother's.

"I remember that your dad told me once that, if anything happened to him, the store would support us."

"Let's talk to Elaine and Janet and see what they say. We'll need everyone's help, and everyone has to be in complete agreement, don't you think?"

"They'll be over soon, and we'll talk then."

"We have to do it, Mom. We have to."

The other two daughters agreed that the store should reopen. They thought it would honor their father if they could keep the family business going. Elaine said she would send Ben to Central Presbyterian's Mother's Day Out, and Janet could leave Sara with her mother-in-law. Tom Ware, Suzanne's husband, offered to help in any way. They decided that Tuesday, September 16th, would be the day they would all go in, if only for an hour or two. Or as long as they could stand it for the first time. They voted to meet at 8:30 a.m.

✳ ✳ ✳ ✳ ✳ ✳

Tuesday morning, they all parked in front of the store. There was no need to save space for customers. Karen handed Tom the keys, and they followed him inside the building. The air conditioning had been turned off, so the store was very hot. It smelled of Clorox. One by one, they walked past the empty showcases and into the back room.

Elaine was the first to turn away, and then Karen. Janet and her mother and Tom stood there for a long time. Then they backed out of the room. They'd all seen the big blood stain that Tommy had not been able to get out of the beige vinyl flooring. At least the stain could not be seen from the front of the store, they were sure of that.

"We can talk to the insurance people. Maybe they will put in a new floor for us," Ruth said. "Let's go home, now."

Janet agreed. "We can try tomorrow."

Elaine wiped her eyes on a Kleenex, one from a box she kept in the car.

"Yes, tomorrow. We'll try tomorrow."

CHAPTER EIGHTEEN

While Chantina Ginn was boarding a Greyhound bus in Florida, the Staton women were beginning their arduous task of taking inventory in earnest. They had walked through the store the previous day, a full week since the robbery and murders of Kenneth Staton and Suzanne Staton Ware. They hadn't stayed more than ten minutes, but on Thursday, the 18th of September, they vowed to stay at least two hours.

Karen detached herself from the tragedy and somehow managed to keep her mind devoted to the numbers on the inventory pages from the past January. She knew that purchases made since that date were added, and sales since that date were subtracted. That meant going through stacks and stacks of receipts. She contacted all their suppliers, and they were kind and considerate of the situation, sent replacement merchandise, and were willing to wait for payment until the insurance claims were settled.

Ruth, Janet, and Elaine counted the merchandise left, while Suzanne's husband, Tom Ware, helped with whatever he was told to do, such as moving glass shelves from the front windows. They had all realized that the shelves filled with decorative items blocked the view of the inside of the store from the street. That was a security risk they wanted to correct immediately.

The generosity of people anxious to help was overwhelming. An expert carpenter, Mark Kesner, showed up one afternoon unannounced. He normally built and installed high-dollar cabinetry in new homes built by his brother, Wimpy. He installed a two-way mirror in the wall so that anyone working in the back room could see out into the main room without being seen.

"It was something I've been thinking about," Mark said, after being thanked by Ruth. "I decided the mirror would be more helpful than sending flowers."

Karen realized that she could remember just about all of the rings that were stolen. During times when she took a break from working on the inventory, she sketched out with pencil the pictures of the rings stolen. At night, when she couldn't sleep, she grabbed her pencil and the index-sized poster board she'd found at the store. She knew, if any of the jewelry was ever recovered, her sketches would be invaluable.

Janet and Elaine were occupied with their two small children and couldn't stay at the store for long. Once, when both were at the Azure house with their children, Garrick Feldman, the editor of *The Press Argus*, called and asked if he could come over and interview them. Both women were reluctant, but they finally agreed since they knew the editor's reputation as a good man and a fine reporter.

They sat in their mother's living room, watching Ben and Sara play on the floor. It was too hot to let them play outside. They asked Feldman in and offered him some iced tea, which he accepted. He began the interview by saying that the whole community grieved for the Staton family. He said Kenneth Staton probably was the most well-liked and respected man in town. And their little sister, Suzanne, was everything a father would want in a daughter.

Elaine said, "My sister was probably my best friend. She was intelligent. A straight-A student. I still think of what Suzy and I might be doing right now."

"My daddy was such a gentle person," Janet added. She also told Feldman that her husband and son were coming the next weekend to get her and daughter, Sara. "We have to go home and try to get some normalcy in our life."

"People have been really great," Elaine said.

Feldman sensed that the interview was hard for the sisters, and they weren't used to being in the spotlight, especially one so tragic. Ever the journalist, he thought of his headline for the column he'd write following the interview: "Distraught Staton Family Continues to Mourn."

When he left, the sisters breathed easier.

"I'm glad that's over," Elaine said. "I really, really do miss Suzy."

Talking about Suzy had made Janet think of the funny story her mother had told the night before after Sara had been put to bed. They had been standing in the kitchen, cleaning up after supper.

"I just remembered something funny about Suzanne when she was a little girl," Ruth had said. She was smiling, and once again, Janet remembered how pretty her mom was when she smiled. "One of my cousins was visiting and said she was going to Seattle. Suzy looked up at me and said, 'Who's Attle?'"

Ruth knew that, from then on, those memories of the simplest of conversations with Suzanne would be the ones she would treasure the most.

Elaine could just imagine that scene, with Suzy looking up so sweetly and innocently into her mother's brown eyes. Suzy was such an easygoing child, and she never needed scolding because she never misbehaved. As a child, she often rode on her daddy's lap as he rolled his wheelchair into Sunday school and church. She adored her daddy, and the terror both of them faced together before they were killed was what saddened Elaine the most.

CHAPTER NINETEEN

There's an old saying that a lawman hot on the trail of a suspect is like a "bird dog on point." And Don Taylor was certainly that bird dog. After talking to the man behind the counter at the Terry Motel, he had the scent, and he was going after it.

Don Taylor now had a name: Damon Peterson. He had his companion's name: Rick. He had the license number of Rick's motorcycle. And Pat Etier had told them that the two were camped out at Horseshoe Bend up on Beaver Lake.

Taylor and Detective Dan Short drove to Rogers and took the bridge at Highway 12 to the lake. After finding the Horseshoe Bend campground and talking to Larry Gray in the camp permit office, Taylor was told that a campsite had been registered to a Pete Hubbard for the 4th, 5th, and 6th of September, but that Hubbard had left suddenly, leaving behind two of his party in 1-9. Those two moved over to a campsite newly registered to Damon Peterson, 1-10, who arrived later on the evening of September 6th.

The campsite was deserted, but they searched the leavings of a recent burn in the fire pit at 1-9. Amongst burned garbage and beer cans, they recovered price tags, a jewelry box, some empty ring boxes, a watch band display holder, and remnants of rope that were similar to that used to tie up Kenneth and Suzanne. And fused to a beer tab was a watch price tag that read $225.00.

And perhaps the biggest find was an Orange Blossom ring display filler used in ring trays if a ring had been sold.

"Hot dog," Taylor said. "Now where did they go?"

Taylor surmised that they'd had to get another car. Other campers said they'd seen an old blue and white Cadillac parked at the campsite, but they'd also seen a mechanic working on it. With that information, Taylor and his men began a canvas of local used car lots, and once again, "Hot Dog!" They talked to a Mr. Jeffcoat at Economy Auto Sales in Rogers, and he did, indeed, trade a Plymouth for a '71 Cadillac.

The Cadillac wasn't worth much, so it was sold to a salvage yard. Taylor went there, found the car, and had it towed to the State Police Headquarters in Fort Smith on Kelly Highway. Inside the car was an assortment of evidence: a map of local campgrounds, a torn page out of a telephone book that had Kenneth Staton's address and phone number on it, and a copy of the September 11th *Northwest Arkansas Morning Times* with headlines of the Staton Jewelry Store robbery.

Taylor put out a description of Damon Peterson and Rick Anderson, noting that they were wanted in conjunction with an armed robbery and murder in Van Buren, Arkansas. He was hopeful that older-model, green Plymouth would give out on them, and they'd be stranded somewhere. He just wished he knew what direction they were headed. He presumed south because of the license tag information and the motel reservation, which told him that Florida and Georgia were home territory. But would they be smart and head north? Robbers and murderers weren't usually smart.

CHAPTER TWENTY

The relentless heat continued, and each day the Staton women went to Cloverleaf Shopping Center to the Staton Jewelry Store. Despite the closed sign on the door, folks would peer in the windows, curiosity seekers mostly. Some even knocked, but the door was never unlocked.

Janet and her little girl, Sara, returned to Paris, Texas. Elaine's little boy missed his almost constant playmate. And the sun rose each morning, as if nothing bad had happened.

Brian Gaines, a jeweler from Fort Smith, contacted Karen and asked if he could be of help. Brian had gone to high school with Suzanne. He arranged to meet with Karen and her mom, and they discussed the best way for the store to open. Brian brought along his assistant, Danny Dyer. They both had excellent references and did work for several stores. They told the ladies that they would pick up and deliver any repairs. Dennis Tolzman was also added to the list of those who would help, primarily because Kenneth Staton was greatly admired by all the jewelers in the area. Dennis Tolzman was an excellent watch repairman, and he was hired to pick up and deliver.

"Mr. Staton was the only jeweler we wished good business to," Brian Gaines said.

Getting the store ready to open was a big challenge. Wounds were so fresh in everyone's hearts that going to the store was like climbing into a deep hole. And sometimes it was hard to climb back out of that hole.

The Staton women were frightened that the murderers might come back and kill them. Men on motorcycles scared them, and once, while Karen was at Safeway, she saw a white van parked at the side of the store. She thought the men could have been in the van, and she ran for her car. She had heard that someone had reported to the police about seeing a mysterious white van at the Sleepy Hollow apartments on September 10th, near the same place where Suzanne's jeep was found.

Elaine's husband worked at night, and she kept a light on in her bedroom until he got home. She could not stop thinking about what she saw that day on the floor in the back room of the jewelry store, and her way of dealing with it was not to talk about it unless she absolutely had to.

Ruth kept thinking that she could have been killed, and she worried constantly about how frightened her husband and daughter must have been. She prayed that they were happy in heaven and didn't remember what had happened to them.

✳ ✳ ✳ ✳ ✳ ✳

The Fort Smith and Van Buren newspapers kept the murders alive by having headlines and stories in every issue. "No Leads Found in Staton Inquiry" was one headline. Another was "Distraught Staton Family Wants the Killer Caught."

Virgil Goff, the chief of police, was quoted as saying, "I want the public to know that we need their cooperation in every way. If they have jewelry at the shop, we need to know about it. If they've seen anything unusual, they need to come forward, and we'll keep the information confidential. You know, many times people don't want to help in an investigation because they're scared the criminals will find out about it. I assure the public that whatever they tell us will remain confidential."

And then Virgil Goff summed up the case: "It was a brutal thing. They were bound and gagged on the floor. They couldn't have been a threat to anybody, and yet the murderers killed them anyway. They were vicious, merciless men, who don't care for the value of a human life."

Mayor Gene Bell also added his two cents' worth: "We seem to be having communication problems with the CID (Criminal Investigation Division with the state police), but that may be because they are on the verge of a breakthrough."

CHAPTER TWENTY-ONE

Rick Anderson was still living in an adjoining motel room on the beach with Damon and Loralei, whose name was really Cindy Sue Brown. She knew her boyfriend/husband, whose real name was Eugene Wallace Perry, was growing tired of her, and she feared he might get rid of her because she knew too much. He'd talked enough, and often, about killing Chantina for that very reason.

Cindy Sue/Loralei had lived in fear of being caught for something illegal most of her life, so she was no stranger to looking out for herself. She was just waiting for the chance to leave Florida.

Rick was drunk most of the time, and he was now wearing a small pistol in a leather ankle holster. He also owned a Colt revolver that he'd bought, along with a shoulder holster. He was an armed dude now, scared at any minute he was going to be arrested for murder in Arkansas. He wanted to get out of the clutches of Peterson, or whatever the hell his name was. Rick bought a white van after Chantina left, and he planned on leaving Florida and heading back to Fayetteville, Arkansas, so he could retrieve his Harley.

The local radio station was airing ads about a new jewelry store opening in Jacksonville Beach, and Damon was already making plans to rob it. Since he'd been so successful with one jewelry store robbery, he was cocky enough to think he could rob another. Damon bought the book *The Anarchist's Cook Book*, which explained how to make a silencer that would fit a .22 automatic. Armed with that knowledge and the tools he needed, Damon insisted that Rick help him.

There was a tavern on the beach next to the motel in the 300 block of Oceanfront South—a rough place that was not visited by families on vacation. Badass dudes and gals frequented the bar, and it was the perfect spot for Rick and Damon and Loralei to hang out and get drunk. Stay drunk, really, was what they all did.

Around 2:30 a.m. on September 23rd, Damon and Loralei left the bar, but Rick Anderson wasn't ready to leave yet. He sat at the bar, drinking and talking to another man and a woman. When he got ready to leave, he could barely climb off the stool, but he headed toward the door. He was jumped by someone trying to rob him, so he reached for his pistol hidden at his ankle. A fight ensued, and the man wrestled the pistol away from him. Rick then ran next door to the motel and banged on Damon's door, which was nearest the tavern. Damon opened the front door for his drunk friend, and Rick grabbed a gun from a bedside table, stood at the open doorway, and fired toward the tavern, at nobody in particular. Damon didn't know what the hell was going on, so he grabbed a gun under his pillow and ran outside. Rick retreated to his adjoining room for a minute and then ran as fast as he could toward the beach in the opposite direction, sobering up a little with each step in the shifting sand.

By that time, the tavern owner had called the police, and they arrived with guns drawn. Armed with a Rossi .38 revolver and a Beretta .25 pistol, Damon headed down the beach the opposite direction from where Rick had run. A shootout with police ensued. Damon was hit in the shoulder and taken to the hospital under arrest for attempted murder because he shot at the police. The hospital was conveniently located not far from the police headquarters.

While the gun battle was going on, Rick Anderson hid behind some oleander bushes. The police shined their spotlights all around, but they didn't see him. He waited a long time until he thought they had left, and then he snuck back to his room to get the keys to his van and escape. Instead, he was met by the police, who were staking out his room.

Rick Anderson, too, was arrested and taken to the police headquarters. He asked for his one phone call and contacted a friend who was in the bail bonding business.

"Call my dad in Lighthouse Point, Florida, and get him to bail me out."

Bail was set at $3,500, so his dad wired $350. Anderson was released before dawn and told to come back for arraignment that afternoon. Instead, he hopped a Greyhound, leaving his dad and his dad's money in the lurch.

In the two motel rooms, police confiscated $2,000 in one-hundred-dollar bills and various items of jewelry. Police also found five handguns and two sawed-off rifles with homemade silencers. They also impounded a 1975 Dodge van recently purchased by Anderson and a 1976 Oldsmobile Cutlass bought in Atlanta by Peterson.

Authorities released names and descriptions on a regional teletype wire after their arrests. The ages of the men were both listed as twenty-five, with Anderson from Topeka, Kansas, and Peterson—now also known as Damon Malantino—from Atlanta, Georgia.

The information reached Arkansas authorities quickly.

The same information reached Georgia authorities.

A woman and her twelve-year-old son, who ran a camping area in Tyrone, Georgia, had been found gagged, bound with rope, and shot execution style only two weeks before the Staton murders.

The crimes were eerily similar.

CHAPTER TWENTY-TWO

On Wednesday, September 24th, Ruth Staton received a telephone call from the chief of police, Virgil Goff.

"Mrs. Staton, we need to come over right now, if that's all right with you."

Ruth replied, "Of course." Then she hung up and told Karen to hurry up and get dressed because something was fixing to happen. "I don't know what, but it sounded urgent. Maybe they've caught them."

Karen quickly pulled on a shirt and shorts. They had already decided that they weren't going down to the store that morning, and Karen had stayed up late sketching the rings that were stolen.

The doorbell rang shortly, and Chief Goff and Assistant Chief Wayne Hicks stood outside. Both men seemed excited. Happy, even.

Everyone sat down at the dining room table, and Goff asked them to look at a line-up of photographs. The first one was identified by Karen.

"That's the one I waited on the Monday before that Wednesday. I recognize his long hair and his teeth. He had white teeth, and he was tanned like this man."

Goff said, "And you saw him on Monday the eighth?"

"Correct."

Ruth identified a picture of a man with blond, curly hair. He was wearing a white shirt of some kind.

"That's him. He came in with a woman and looked at wedding rings. He stayed a long time, and that made me kind of nervous. Suzanne came from around back and stood by me."

Shortly after the women gave a positive identifications, Ron Fields and Doug Stephens with the Arkansas State Police arrived.

Ron Fields looked at Karen and said, "Will you fly down to Florida with us to Jacksonville Beach? We want to see if you can identify some jewelry we've found. You'd know it better than anyone."

Karen's heart pounded with fright.

"Oh, I don't know if I can or not."

"You will be perfectly safe. We'll be with you all the time."

Karen looked at her mother, and her mother's eyes teared up.

"You can do it, Karen. I know you can. You have to. Nobody left knows the jewelry inventory like you do," she said, immediately regretting the way she had phrased it.

Karen was still hesitant. She'd suffered so much already. Finally, she said she'd go. She did know the stock. Better than anyone alive.

"Good!" Fields said. "We've already booked a flight for early tomorrow morning. It should be a quick trip, but be prepared to stay two days, just in case."

That night, Karen packed her bag with a blue-and-white dress, white shorts, navy shirt, jeans, sweatshirt, and blue tennis shoes. She would wear a black-and-white print dress and white sandals on the plane. In her small black purse she carried for dress occasions, she tucked in her billfold, a small hairbrush, and two small packs of Kleenex. She figured she'd need them.

Even though the police offered to drive her to the airport, her mother said she would. Karen was booked on a 7:00 a.m. flight, so they left Van Buren around 5:30. They didn't want to be late.

On the drive over, Karen said, "Mother, I'm so nervous."

Ruth was nervous also, but she wanted to concentrate on her driving. She didn't drive to the airport in Fort Smith often enough to really know the way. She decided to just go the way she'd go if she was visiting her mother's house and take the Greenwood exit.

"Mom, is this the quickest way?"

"This is the way I'm most comfortable."

"Well, we sure don't want to get lost."

Ruth smiled and with her right hand patted Karen's.

"This way I know we won't for sure."

They discussed the reopening of the store and the ring holders that hadn't arrived yet.

"You know, Karen," her mother said, "we can't open without you."

"I know, Mother. I won't be gone more than two days. I doubt that long. Ron Fields just said to prepare for two days."

When they reached the airport, parked, and walked to the terminal, they felt a cool breeze.

"Wow, Mother, feel that breeze."

"Yes, maybe we're going to finally get some relief."

As the slap of Karen's sandals echoed across the parking lot pavement, her mom thought about that word: *relief.* The word echoed in Ruth's mind. Would finding the killers bring them relief? Would it be immediate? Or would it never come?

When they arrived at the gate, greetings were passed between the Staton women and the law enforcement officers. Ron Fields told the ladies that Sheriff Ball, Wayne Hicks, Dan Short, and a man from CIS had already left by car for Florida and would meet them there.

Karen hugged her mother goodbye and boarded the Delta Airlines plane that would fly first to Atlanta, and then they'd transfer to another plane to go on to Jacksonville.

Karen sat next to Doug Stephens.

"I know this is frightening for you," he said. "But we'll be with you all the time. It's very traumatic, of course, and we recognize that. Please don't feel embarrassed about being scared."

"Who are these guys, and how did you find them?" Karen asked.

"Well, there was a shootout between police and two men down in Jacksonville Beach. One, a man who has several aliases, was shot in the shoulder, and he's in custody in the hospital there. The other one, a young guy named Rick Anderson, the man you identified, posted bond but skipped out, so he's long gone."

"How did that happen?"

"Because they didn't have anything major to hold Anderson on. He didn't fire on the police like the other man did. And he didn't get shot in the arm."

Stephens rubbed his hands together, like a man preparing to eat a big steak. He continued, "That man that was shot was wearing two rings when he was arrested, and they found some cash and guns and jewelry in their motel room."

"Oh, I hope they've got the right ones," Karen said.

"They found evidence in a car also."

The stewardess came by with peanuts and a drink for everybody. Stephens nodded his head yes, but Karen couldn't think about eating peanuts or drinking a Coke.

"Goodness, no," she said.

By the time they arrived in Jacksonville, Karen was exhausted. She wasn't comfortable in planes anyway, and all the time in the air she felt like she might throw up at any minute.

When the Jacksonville Beach police met them, they ushered them to a waiting police car, and they drove forty minutes to Jacksonville Beach. From there they were driven directly to the hospital where they were ushered into a small room, more like an office than a meeting room.

Karen listened to the hum of the air conditioning unit that must have been right outside their room. On the loud-speaker system, voices asked Doctors So-and-So to call various numbers. Shortly, a young woman arrived and laid two rings on a table.

Karen gasped and felt nauseous. One ring belonged to her daddy. The other one had been in their display case.

Fields watched Karen's face turn white. He turned to Stephens, and Fields saw him lift his chin and nod his head yes.

After a minute or two of complete silence, Fields asked her if she was okay. Karen assured him that she was, but she'd like some water because the room was suddenly spinning.

"This ring is Daddy's wedding band," she said, pointing to one. She felt dizzy, and for a second, she thought she might faint.

Fields asked how she could be sure. "Was there an engraving?"

"No, but there would be a Vellmar trademark stamped inside. Will you look? I don't think I can," Karen said.

Doug Stephens picked up the ring and turned it over a time or two. "It's there."

Standing up to leave the room, Ron Fields said, "I'd better make sure we've got a couple of guards on that hospital room. I'll be right back."

Doug Stephens pointed to the other ring. "And this one?"

"That came from the store." She saw dried blood encrusted on the ring, and she thought it must be her daddy's. "Is that Daddy's blood?"

"Oh, no. The man who got shot by the police was wearing it. It's his blood."

Karen looked at it closer. It was identical to the one they'd had in stock. In fact, it was one she had recently sketched called the "Star of Africa." She took a long breath.

"This is just like the one we carried."

Ron Fields quickly returned and said, "I know how difficult this is for you. You've been a tremendous help. There are a few more pieces of jewelry at the police department we need you to identify. They came out of these guys' motel rooms."

They were then taken to police headquarters, which was just minutes away, and there Karen identified a Longines brand watch and a "Star of Africa" nugget-style diamond wedding band, both identical to what they sold at their store. There were also four gold coins that Ruth Staton had kept in the safe as mementos.

Doug Stephens stayed with Karen while Ron Fields left to attend to some legal matters. When he returned, a Jacksonville Beach policeman drove them back to a motel where they had reservations waiting.

Both men walked her to her room.

"We'll give you time to rest," Ron said. "Maybe you can take a little nap or take a shower. When you're ready, you can call us, and we'll go eat. Don't be scared at all. You're perfectly safe."

Karen was so upset that she certainly could not take a nap. She did take a shower. She thought that might help her to relax. And it did, a little. She put on shorts and a shirt, which were more comfortable in the Florida sticky heat. She also pulled her hair up and fastened it with a gold clasp she'd brought from home.

When they arrived at the restaurant, she recognized Sheriff Trellon Ball and Wayne Hicks, and she felt better seeing kind and familiar faces from home. They stood up when she entered.

"You're doing a real good job, Karen," the sheriff said. He hugged her softly. "Your mama will be real proud of you."

There at the restaurant were two officers from Georgia. They were investigating the robbery and murder at a campground in Tyrone, Georgia, which was very similar to the one in Van Buren.

"It was a woman and her twelve-year-old son. They even killed their dog."

The conversations at the table centered around the two crimes. Even though nearly everyone at the table order seafood, Karen ordered a salad, which she had trouble eating—not because it wasn't good, but because she was afraid she wouldn't be able to keep it down.

Ron Fields was able to get warrants for both men for capital murder. They were identified as Richard Phillip Anderson, age twenty-three, and Damon Malantino, also known as Damon Peterson, who was not the same age as Anderson, but nearer thirty-six.

Fields and Karen flew back to Fort Smith on Friday afternoon, and Doug Stephens stayed behind to assist in the investigation. On the return flight, Ron Fields kept telling Karen what a tremendous help she was. She should be really proud of herself, and that he understood how hard it was to look at her daddy's ring.

"Just know that you were a big part of solving this crime. That's got to make you feel good about finding your daddy's and sister's killers."

He went on to say that he had called a press conference for when they got back to Fort Smith.

"No one should be there when we arrive because nobody knows when we're scheduled to land."

As they deplaned and walked through the terminal, Karen heard someone call her name. It scared her, and she was afraid she'd be facing the press, who'd ask a lot of questions.

Instead, it was Warren MacLellan, who was a pilot for Frontier Airlines and was just arriving from a flight.

"Everything okay?" he asked.

Karen was relieved when she realized the voice belonged to Warren. She hugged his blue uniform jacket and said, "I've been down to Florida to identify some jewelry, Warren. I think they've caught the men who did it."

"Wonderful," he said. "I'll be sure to tell Wanda. Be sure to tell your mom to call us if she needs us for anything. Anything at all."

Karen smiled and waved goodbye. She had a store to open, and she needed to get home and see her family.

Home. That was what was most important to her right that minute.

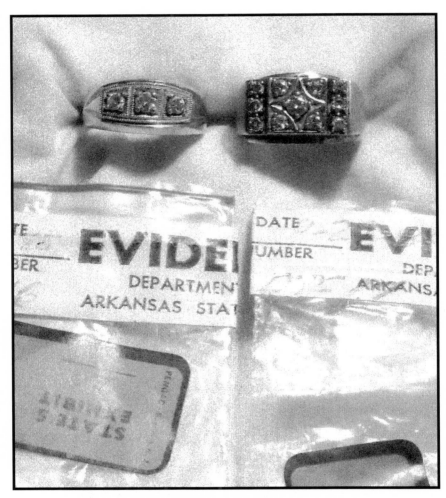

JEWELRY IDENTIFIED BY KAREN IN FLORIDA

CHAPTER TWENTY-THREE

On the Monday after Karen and Ron Fields returned from Florida, Don Taylor received a call from a self-storage owner in Fayetteville, a Mr. Gifford Heckathorn. He reported that he had signed a lease agreement on September 11th, 1980, with a man who signed his name Damon Peterson on the contract. Another man was with him, riding a motorcycle. They rented space 109 for a month.

Mr. Heckathorn went on to say that the first reason for calling the police was that a Mr. William Anderson had called and said he was coming to remove the contents of the storage unit. His brother had skipped bond in Florida that their father had provided, so he was going to take the trailer and the motorcycle back to Topeka, Kansas, as a way of payment to their father.

Taylor thanked the storage owner and proceeded to seek permission to search the contents of the storage unit. Municipal Judge Lawson Cloninger issued the search warrant, and Taylor and his men took off for Fayetteville.

There they found the camper, the Harley-Davidson motorcycle, and two black motorcycle helmets. As they were looking through the camper, Mr. William B. Anderson arrived with a wrecker capable of hauling the camper and motorcycle back to Kansas. He told Taylor the same story: his brother Richard Phillip Anderson had been arrested in Jacksonville Beach, Florida, and had jumped bond. He also told the detective that Richard had told his father that Damon Peterson was dangerous and was linked to the Mafia and for them to be cautious.

After taking careful notes of a lengthy conversation with the Anderson brother as to where everyone lived and worked, Taylor said, "Well, looks like you made this trip for nothing. And it also looks like your brother is in a heap of trouble. And for that, I'm sorry for you and your dad."

The trailer and motorcycle were taken back to police headquarters in Fort Smith and examined thoroughly. Attached to the bumper was a cardboard license that read "Lost Tag."

Inside the pop-up camper, among many other items, they found a gold coin, a buffalo nickel with a nick on its face, a jewelry price tag with Karen Staton's handwriting, an Orange Blossom ring filler, a book of matches from the Terry Motel, a book of matches from the Horseshoe Bend Marina in Rogers, a black Harley-Davidson motorcycle jacket, a man's suit, a woman's coat, jeans, and heat hair curlers. There were also sleeping bags and dirty sheets. All of these items were bagged and labeled separately.

Don Taylor took pictures of the motorcycle, believed to be the same color and make as the one that Damon Peterson and Richard Anderson were seen riding in the vicinity of the Cloverleaf Shopping Center and the Staton Jewelry Store. The men and their motorcycle were even identified by police who regularly kept watch over the Terry Motel, which was known to police as a haven for down-and-outers and criminals.

Taylor and his men were elated.

"Great detective work, men," they were told by the entire law enforcement community.

The date was September 27th, 1980.

Now, to find Anderson and get Peterson out of the hospital and see where they stood with bringing the bastards to trial.

CHAPTER TWENTY-FOUR

On September 30th, 1980, the Fort Smith *Southwest Times Record* reported that capital murder warrants had been issued for Richard Phillip Anderson, age twenty-three, of Topeka, Kansas, and Damon Malantino, thirty-six, alias Damon Peterson, of Atlanta, Georgia. These warrants were for the murders of Kenneth Staton and Suzanne Staton Ware.

Also, it was reported that these same men were wanted for the murders of a woman and her son at a campsite known as Camper's Paradise in Tyrone, Georgia, on August 25th, 1980.

The city editor reported in another column that Ron Fields revealed in a press conference that there had been a gun battle at a Jacksonville Beach, Florida, tavern that resulted in the arrest of two men. One suspect, Damon Malantino, alias Peterson, was injured in the shoulder by a police bullet and was currently under police watch at a Jacksonville hospital. The other suspect, Richard Anderson, made bond but failed to show up for his arraignment the following day. He was considered armed and dangerous.

* * * * * *

At the age of twenty-three, Richard Anderson was in the most trouble of his life. An alcoholic, a twice-divorced husband, a father of a little girl being raised by his parents, a former owner of a dating service, a pimp, and a biker who rode Harleys and kept a knife strapped to his ankle, he was not the boy his parents had hoped he would be.

His father was an engineer for IBM in New York, and that is where his family lived when Anderson was born. He had an older brother and two sisters. His mom was a stay-at-home mom, and they were devout Seventh Day Adventists. He was affectionately called Rick.

Rick had attended ninth grade in Union Springs, New York, at Union Springs Academy, a Seventh Day Adventist School. On spring break in 1972, he came home to his family in Topeka, Kansas, where his father had been transferred. He'd purchased some pot, took it back to school, and was busted. Dismissed from the academy, his parents had enrolled him in public school in Topeka.

In the tenth grade, Rick had started skipping school and hanging out with an older eighteen-year-old guy and a girl named Holly, who had gotten busted with some LSD. Rick and Holly hooked up. The older guy cashed in some savings bonds belonging to his father, and he and his girlfriend bought a van and planned to go to Texas, where it was warm. After leaving a note on the kitchen table for his parents, Rick bought two cases of beer, and he and Holly set off on a big adventure with their friends. The year was 1976, at the height of free love and drugs and yellow vans and Woodstock and thumbs-down on traditional life in the USA.

At Texarkana, Texas, their van broke down, and they took a Greyhound to Corpus Christi, Texas, where they rented an apartment. They invited a married couple to live with them. The wife turned tricks to support their heroin habit.

It was in Texas that Ricky turned sixteen and could be officially labeled an alcoholic—and already in deep shit.

Now, in late September of 1980, he was twenty-three, on the run in Florida, knowing that it was just a matter of days before the pieces of the puzzle would be put together by the police and he'd be arrested for the robbery and murders in Van Buren, Arkansas.

He'd taken a cab to the bus station in Jacksonville Beach and gone to Fort Lauderdale. He hid out at a friend's house and told him about his trouble in Arkansas and Florida. His friend, Johnny, was a knowledge-able man in his sixties, who offered to let Ricky ride on the next plane trip he would make to South America to bring back drugs. He advised Rick to leave the country, but Rick knew that, if he went to South America, he couldn't speak the language. So instead, Johnny told him how to escape to Canada. He told Rick to fly to Detroit and purchase a two-way bus ticket to Canada. A one-way ticket would have caused suspicion. Rick followed his advice.

When the border officials had boarded the bus, they checked Rick's two-way ticket and asked how long he was going to stay.

"About a week," Rick said.

It turned out to be much longer than that.

When Rick stepped off the bus in Toronto, he located a hostel, an inexpensive place to stay. He called his father in Lighthouse Point, Flor-ida, to tell him where he was. His father told him he was in big trouble, and that he was wanted in Arkansas in connection with a robbery and murder.

Rick told his father, "Well, I guess you won't be seeing me for a long while."

Desperate now, and feeling guilty over disappointing his father and causing him such anguish, Rick headed for an Army Surplus Store. Because he had grown up in upstate New York, he knew what winter weather was like, and he knew winter was setting in. He'd need the proper clothing for hiding out in Canada. He purchased heavy white snow boots, warm pants, a parka, and an equipped backpack with the

Canadian red-and-green emblem stitched on the back. The owner offered him a job helping to clean out a warehouse, so he stayed there and worked for about a week.

Knowing he should always keep moving, he took off with a guy he met at the hostel where he was staying. The man suggested they try picking mushrooms in Alberta, so off they went. Another adventure for a good-looking young man who was digging his grave of shit deeper and deeper.

* * * * * *

While Rick Anderson was walking across Canada, hitching rides, always looking over his shoulder and taking odd jobs to survive, Damon Peterson was plotting his plan to escape a murder charge in both Arkansas and Georgia.

His first defense was that his real name was Eugene Wallace Perry, and he had never been in Van Buren, Arkansas, in his life. His only connection with Damon Peterson and Rick Anderson was that he was the fence they used to sell the stolen jewelry. He was in Oxford, Alabama, at the time of the crimes in Arkansas, visiting with his family, and he had witnesses to prove it: his two teenage daughters, Dawn and Tonya; his ex-wife, Glenda Perry; his father and mother, Wallace and Eulene; and a few scattered friends.

When he was arrested in Jacksonville Beach during the shootout at the tavern, the police seized his personal property, which included over $2,000 in cash, one diamond studded wedding band, one diamond studded ring, one man's gray suit, one man's sport coat, one man's dress hat, six pairs of men's trousers, six men's dress shirts, five men's T-shirts, two pairs of men's cowboy boots, two pairs of men's shoes, one suitcase, one hanging garment bag, and assorted underwear and shorts. Clearly, one could reasonably call Wallace Eugene Perry a clotheshorse. He also had a fondness for cigars, as evidenced in photographs of Perry eventually published in newspapers when he did finally go to trial.

He also had a four page rap sheet of various offenses, such as robbery, possession of stolen property, possession of controlled substances, and distribution of narcotics in Georgia, Tennessee, and Alabama. He'd been imprisoned, paroled, fined. Also included were a long list of aliases: Damon Malantino, Damon Peterson, Jim Jackson, Eugene Wallace Hubbard, and Marvin Allen Williams.

Perry was born in Ohio on July 8th, 1944, but grew up in Gadsden and Oxford Alabama, two nearby towns in northern Alabama. He worked in construction, was the father of two daughters, and was divorced from their mother. In one Alabama arrest, he had threatened to cut off the fingers of a man's son if the man didn't tell him where some money was hidden. He claimed to have made over $150,000 in drug dealings in 1979.

Eugene Perry and Cindy Sue Brown (aka Loralei) hooked up sometime before 1980, probably by a mutual involvement with the drug scene in the Atlanta region. Cindy had been arrested in Gadsden, Alabama, for possession of controlled substances in October of 1979 and in Atlanta in May of 1980, where she was sentenced to thirty-six months probation.

Perhaps Cindy Sue liked Perry's green eyes, and he liked her cute little figure. Even while he was in prison in Florida, he wrote to Cindy's grandmother, confessing his love for Cindy Sue, and when he was paroled, they hooked up again. Cindy Sue claimed she was afraid of Perry, and that he had conned her into falling in love with him.

In Tyrone, Georgia, a little town south of Atlanta, at Camper's Paradise, they had lived together for about three months in a trailer, which was located near the camp office. Perry also owned a blue and white Cadillac and a pop-up camper, which he parked next to the trailer. Many of the fellow campers believed Cindy Sue and Perry were married, or at least living together as a couple. However, Perry also was off and on romantically involved with Barbara Price, a fellow camper and the office manager, who collected the rent. She also had a twelve-year-old son, who sometimes lived with her.

Barbara Price had known that a big van show was coming to stay at the campground for about a week. She'd told Perry that, if he stayed a week longer than when he was planning to leave, he could sell a lot of drugs to the bikers, and that she would take a small percentage of the profits Perry would make.

Perry stayed and made money. So did Barbara Price.

On August 25th, she and her son were found gagged and tied up with rope and each murdered by two shots to the head.

Perry claimed he left Paradise on August 20th, 1980. He'd need plenty of excuses and several more aliases to get out of trouble in Georgia and in Arkansas.

CHAPTER TWENTY-FIVE

Karen Staton had set her alarm for 6:30 a.m. on the 28th of September, but she waked before it sounded. She had taken her bath the night before and planned the dress and sandals she'd wear to the first day of reopening the jewelry store. With the stoic resignation she had exhibited since she and her mother had made the decision to reopen, she climbed out of bed and went into the bathroom down the hall.

Her mother was already up and had the coffee ready. She, too, displayed a strong, silent countenance, and tears were not going to fall that day.

Opening the store was something they must do. It was necessary for their survival, both physical and mental. The Christmas catalogue was being printed and would arrive sometime in mid-November, and they had to be ready. As in most retail businesses, Christmas was make or break time.

Ruth offered her daughter some toast and bacon, but she declined, saying she wasn't hungry. She drank a little coffee, kissed her mama's cheek, and went out the kitchen door.

The short drive to Cloverleaf Plaza in her Camaro was such a familiar one, she realized when she parked her car under a parking lot light that she didn't actually remember it. The walk to the store took about twenty-five steps, and when she reached the front door, she had the key ready in her hand. She took a deep breath and unlocked the door.

The store seemed so empty. Until the replacement jewelry arrived, the display cases would have to be filled with something. Having no rings or watches or chains or pendants beckoning customers to take a look would do nothing for the morale of those who worked there or those who came to shop. The insurance company and their suppliers had been extremely helpful in getting claims processed and orders filled, and Karen expected the mail run to be heavy on the first day back.

Phyllis, their part-time employee who was determined to stay with them, arrived shortly before nine, and Karen assigned her the task of calling people whose watches had been repaired and needed to be picked up. Most of their customers knew about the robbery and would be understanding about the delay in notification. Thank goodness, the robbers had left the repair box alone.

Edwin Vinson, the manager of Hunt's Department Store, came over midmorning, bringing cinnamon rolls one of the girls from Hunt's had baked that morning.

"We thought you might enjoy these with your coffee," he said. They were still warm. "Suzanne had put some fall clothes in layaway," he said, his voice dropping to almost a whisper. He handed Karen an envelope. "Her money and receipt are in here."

Karen glanced at the receipt. Suzanne had picked out a pair of brown corduroy pants, a brown plaid cotton blouse, and a burnt-orange sweater. Those colors were in for fall, and Karen remembered Suzanne telling her about the cute things she had bought for the first cool October days.

"Thanks, Edwin," she said. Karen did not allow her eyes to fill with tears. She knew she must protect herself and detach. That was the only way she could survive. "I'll give this to Tom."

Around 11:00 a.m., Ruth arrived for work, feeling somewhat comforted after spending an hour or so in her kitchen reading the sympathy cards and letters that had been arriving since September 11th. One letter in particular pleased her. It was dated September 15th, 1980, and typed on Westark Community College stationery from an English teacher who knew Suzanne.

> *Dear Mrs. Staton,*
> *I would like to express the deep sorrow that I feel for the loss of your husband and daughter. I knew Suzanne as a student in my English class the spring semester of this last school year at Westark Community College. Suzanne made a strong impression on me, not only because of her superior ability as a student, but because of her personality. She has been the only student that I have had who made straight-A's all semester. Also, I was impressed with her modesty and kindness. She was a real asset in the classroom. I know that she and her father are a great loss to their family and their community.*
> *Sincerely,*
> *Joy Lowe, Chairman*
> *Division of Humanities*

As any mother would, Ruth felt pleased to read the gracious words about her Suzanne. She did make a mark in the world in which she lived. And if she had lived, she would have accomplished whatever she wanted to do. Ruth felt confident about that. Suzanne's English teacher said so.

Ruth chatted with Phyllis about the cards she'd received in the mail.

"You wouldn't believe how many we've gotten," she said. "It will take me forever to read them all, and I can only read a few at a time."

Phyllis smiled and hugged Ruth.

"Karen has me calling people about their watches. Each person wants to tell me how sorry they are and how much they liked Mr. Staton."

"Oh, that's nice, but it might take you all day if you have to talk to each person."

Ruth walked over to Karen. "What shall I do first?" she asked.

"Well, the mail needs to be opened and boxes unpacked."

"Okay, I'll get right on it," Ruth said.

Karen would be carrying the full load now, but her mother was confident she could do it. Karen was their firstborn, and she had always achieved what she set out to do, even early on when she'd been playing outdoors making mud pies.

The phone rang, and even though Karen stood next to it, she could not answer it. She felt like her throat was closing up, and a surge of panic fill her chest.

"Phyllis, can you get the phone? I've just remembered something I must do or I'll forget it."

"Sure," Phyllis said.

It wasn't until she was home that night and telling her husband about the first day back after the murders that she realized Karen had not once answered the phone all day.

During those first days, Karen did not attempt to answer the ringing telephone. It reminded her of that Wednesday evening when she'd lifted up the phone to call an ambulance but instead had fallen on her knees to the floor and left the phone dangling, the dial tone echoing Karen's own weeping that had come tumbling out in gulps.

* * * * * *

The days passed, merchandise arrived, and shelves were beginning to be stocked with sparkling gold and silver bracelets and rings. Wedding sets beckoned newly engaged couples, and each day was a little bit easier than before.

Merchants from throughout the shopping center stopped by to check on the Statons and give them encouragement. One man in particular, Stan Steele, who operated a radio station, was particularly helpful. With his radio voice that was especially soothing, he passed along the news from the stores, the temperature expected by midday, and how great the Pointers football team was coming along.

But one day was particularly hard. Two women entered the store and looked all around. Karen had seen them before. Van Buren was a small town with lots of familiar-looking people whose names she didn't know. One lady leaned over the counter by the cash register and peered all around.

"Wonder where the bodies were?" she said.

Karen looked at the woman, smiled only slightly, and said, "The bodies were my father and sister."

The women left—not in a huff, but rather like shamed dogs with their tails between their legs.

CHAPTER TWENTY-SIX

Rick and his mushroom-gathering friend hitchhiked to Alberta, with a stop made in Sault Ste. Marie, Ontario, where they slept outside on a pile of rocks and shivered all night in the cold. Another ride took them to Regina, Saskatchewan, where a kind person invited them inside his house for showers and food.

In Alberta, Rick split from his companion because the guy wanted to pick close to the U.S. border, and Rick didn't want to get that close to chances of getting captured. Instead, he went on to Edmonton, where he got a job washing windows from scaffolds on tall buildings. That lasted two weeks, just long enough to get him enough money to move on.

Uneasy about staying too long in one place, he worked for a month at a local moving and storage company. He then moved farther north around Fort St. John, thinking he'd find work in the oil fields, which were somewhere up in the bush down logging roads. These treks were by foot, and Rick was getting more and more exhausted.

He stopped for the night in the open country, thinking he should try to sleep in a tree, but that turned out to be impossible, so he climbed down and gathered some firewood for a night on the ground. His fire went out, and it was too dark to gather more. He listened to wolves howling in the distance and prayed for daylight to come soon.

In the morning, he continued on his journey on foot to the oil rig only to find it had shut down because of political fights between Prime Minister Pierre Trudeau and the oil companies. Only a skeleton crew was left, but he was fed and given a ride back to the nearest town.

He went back to Edmonton and met a man named Joel LaPlant, who was a lowlife, like Rick. LaPlant allowed him to use his name and social insurance number to get a photo ID made. Because the weather was almost blizzard-like in Edmonton, Rick went to Calgary, where he'd been told the weather wasn't as bad. There he stayed at a hostel and met a man named Ivo Shapox. He and Rick went out drinking at night, spending all the money he made in day labor jobs. During one drinking spree, Rick stole Ivo's birth certificate, and using his ID, he hired on with an oil company and spent time out in the field.

Rick was always moving. Always drinking. Always looking over his shoulder. With each move he made, the more desperate he became, and all feelings of self-worth were gone. He felt like he was on the end of a long, long trail.

He remembered the warm living room of his home in upstate New York with his parents and siblings. He could almost smell the salt air of the Atlantic when he and his father took out the sailboat and imagined the warm water on his back as they scuba dove in Florida. His father and brother had tried everything to get Rick back in the arms of his family and back on track to lead a decent life. It wasn't to be, and he was nothing but a drunk, a druggie, and a pimp. Rick found it hard to climb up out of the gutter and much easier to stay down amongst the slime.

Rick was in this frame of mind on December 9th, almost three months to the day after the Arkansas crime, when he arrived in Vancouver after working in a bakery and a small ski resort in Alberta. He found a cheap room and went out to a crowded tavern for a beer. When he was approached at the bar by an older man, who was trying to pick him up, he realized he was in a gay bar. Had he realized what kind of bar it was, he wouldn't have entered because he had a deep disdain for gays.

However, since he was already there, he thought he'd just play along until the time was right.

"I'm going to get us a room," the man said.

"Okay," Rick said and followed him out the door.

The man walked half a block up the street and into the Broadway Hotel. He registered at the desk and asked for two keys. He then went back outside to the street and gave Rick the key to room 312.

After a five minute or so wait, Rick walked into the hotel and pushed the elevator button for the third floor. He knocked on 312, and he was invited in by the overweight, balding man in his fifties. He wore an expensive suit and well-polished shoes. He took off his silk tie and unbuttoned his shirt.

Rick was repulsed by homosexuals. In his opinion, they should all be strangled at the moment of birth, but there he was in a room with a fat queer who probably had a lot of cash on him. He'd play along for a few seconds and then rob the guy.

"You're new at this, aren't you?" the man said.

He moved closer and touched Rick's cheek with his soft hand. He wore an onyx ring on his little finger.

"You might be surprised and like it."

When he felt the man's finger on his face, Rick exploded with rage. The days of living like an animal, foraging for food and shelter and beer, had taken every bit of human compassion out of him. No shred of the cute little Anderson boy was left. He had disgraced his mother and father.

It was then that Rick pulled out a four-inch Buck knife, with the intent of threatening the man. Instead, he stabbed the man in the gut, surprised at how hard it was to kill him. He was fat, and it was excruciatingly difficult to find his vital organs with the short blade. He repeatedly jabbed and probed until the man fell to the floor. Rick didn't even know the man's name until ten years later when he was charged with the murder of a Toronto business executive, Michael John Hendy.

CHAPTER TWENTY-SEVEN

Rick returned to his rented room. Killing a man with a four-inch knife was difficult, and he felt exhausted from the sheer physical strength it took to stab a struggling man. Without taking off his shoes, he fell asleep across the sagging mattress with dirty sheets, a fitting bed for a lowlife like Rick Anderson.

When Rick waked, he evaluated his situation. He had gone beyond the point of no return. He was on the run from the killings in Arkansas, which would result, probably, in the death penalty for him if he was ever caught. His life had never been the same since he met Damon Peterson, and he would be on the run forever. Nothing mattered anymore.

He found a job washing dishes at a high-class Vancouver international hotel, where much of the staff was able to speak multiple languages. As he was wont to do, he left there after a few weeks and decided to return to Edmonton. For that trip, he went by train and traveled through the Rocky Mountains, where it snowed most of the way. The train arrived at the Edmonton station during a blizzard.

He had met a man in an earlier trip to Edmonton, so he walked all the way to the drinking buddy's apartment. His friend had moved, but he was able to break into a nearby unrented room. He stayed there while he looked for his friend. With the blizzard not letting up and no luck in finding his friend, he decided to go to Calgary, where he hoped to find better weather. The weather was just as bad there, so he took another bus back to Vancouver.

As always, the first thing Rick did when he got into a town like Vancouver was head for a bar, where he could always get loaded and meet a woman if he wanted to. At that particular bar, he met a woman named Edith, who was on parole for robbing a bank.

A seed was planted in Rick's inebriated brain that maybe he, too, could rob a bank. It so happened that his rented room's window looked out on a bank, and every time he looked out the window, he saw the bank.

But instead of robbing it, he moved again to a room in Chinatown, north of downtown Vancouver. At a bar, he saw a girl he had met earlier in Edmonton, who was waitressing there. He invited her to go home with him after work, but because his room had no television, she declined. Instead, she introduced him to her friends, who invited Rick to go out with them to live in the bush. He thought that idea sounded good, particularly since the girl was pretty cute, but he needed some cash to get supplies gathered up. He told the girl he was working on something, and he'd let her know in a couple of days.

For the next few days, he holed up in his room, drinking a case of beer he had stolen off a beer truck. With the lucidity and high mentality only alcohol can supply a drunk, he began his plot to rob a bank.

CHAPTER TWENTY-EIGHT

On a stereo brought from Karen's home, music from favorite Christmas albums drifted throughout the Staton Jewelry Store. In an effort to make the store inviting to customers, Karen and Phyllis had begun decorating for Christmas during the week of Thanksgiving. Gold and silver tinsel strands hung across the front windows, and decorative gift items, like silver trays and tea services and glass decanters and silver goblets, sat on sheets of white, fluffy cotton that looked like snow.

Ruth sang along with the music and found she carried a tune better if she sang along with recordings than if she sang by herself.

Tom Ware's brother, Phil, who lived in Denver, had made rum cakes and sent one to Tom, who brought it to the store. But the rum smell was so invasive that nobody wanted to even taste it. Customers also brought trays of cookies and brownies and, of course, the obligatory Christmas fruit cakes.

Everybody was trying their damndest to get through Christmas.

Following a long tradition, the Staton store employees met for breakfast on Christmas Eve morning at the Farmer's Co-Op Restaurant. Nobody went there for the lovely décor because there was none. They went for the good food served from a menu or from a long buffet of scrambled eggs, sausages, bacon, ham, biscuits, gravy, pancakes, waffles, warm syrup, and plenty of grits that everyone, farmers and city-folk alike, enjoyed.

It was the kind of place where people patted their stomachs from being full and stuck a toothpick in their mouth simply because there was a toothpick holder by the cash register and they'd always done so, just like their mother and dad before them. Men in overalls sat in booths or tables with men who wore white shirts and ties, or hunters who'd returned from an early quail hunt, or truck drivers on their last haul before reaching their warm living rooms where their family waited. The waitresses' names were Betty or Carol or Wilma, and they knew their tips would be larger than usual because it was Christmas Eve.

Back at the store after breakfast, Christmas Eve was also the busiest day for men to come to the jewelry store to do their shopping. Many brought the Christmas catalog with them with an item circled by their wives.

"I need that one," one husband said, pointing to a diamond watch, and when told it was still available, a smile crossed his face.

And then came the inevitable question: "How much?" Sometimes the smile remained, and the circled item was boxed and wrapped with the prettiest paper and red bow Staton's could offer. If a smile disappeared, a slightly cheaper alternative was offered, and because it was Christmas Eve, after all, a sales ticket was written up. Husbands were the easiest customers.

Some of the customers during that Christmas season had never shopped there before. They included the various policeman and detectives and prosecutors who had become such an integral part of the Staton family.

Other customers were men who had previously come to Kenneth Staton to inspect and set their Hamilton pocket watches, which was a rule for railroad men to keep the exact time. Even though many had long since retired, they still liked to come just for the reminder of bygone years, when they were young and strong and vibrant. They had liked to visit with Kenneth Staton, and since he wasn't here now, they still felt like coming in and paying their respects.

As closing time arrived that Christmas Eve of 1980, Ruth stood at the front of the store, following the normal procedures of removing the rings from the counters and carrying them into the back room where the safes were located.

As she walked through the door to the back, all of a sudden, she looked up at the wall across from her and saw an image of her husband. There was no pain on his radiant face, and she was sure he no longer suffered from the arthritis that had plagued him for thirty years. He appeared happy, and for the first time since his and Suzanne's deaths, Ruth felt some relief. At that moment, on Christmas Eve, Ruth experienced an epiphany of great magnitude: God had taken care of Kenneth and Suzanne, and He was going to take care of those left.

She carried that feeling home with her, where the family gathered— minus Kenneth and Suzanne, of course. It was a tradition that, on Christmas Eve, they ate pizza from the Pizza Hut and passed out gifts to those whose names were drawn earlier. Janet and her family were in from Paris, Texas. Elaine and Bill and little Ben were there and would celebrate Ben's second birthday on December 26th.

When Tom stood up in front of the multi-colored lit tree that Karen had decorated for her mother, he cleared his throat and fought back tears. Of course, he was thinking of his beautiful, brown-eyed Suzanne on the first Christmas without her. He looked across the room at her sisters, each with the same beautiful brown eyes they'd inherited from their daddy. He braved a smile and passed out small, individually wrapped gift boxes to each of Suzanne's sisters. Jewelry that had belonged to Suzanne was now theirs. A tiny 14-karat-gold serpentine bracelet for Janet. The small gold cross necklace Suzanne always wore belonged now to Elaine. Tiny hoop earrings for Karen. Included in the boxes were notes written by Tom that read: *For being close by* and *For accepting me as me.*

Unfortunately, Suzanne's watch and wedding ring had been stolen from her by Richard Phillip Anderson and Eugene Wallace Perry and had not been recovered.

CHAPTER TWENTY-NINE

January 1st, 1981, arrived warm in the Jacksonville Beach County Jail where Eugene Wallace Perry was residing. He was in a heap of trouble with three counts of attempted murder in Florida, robbery and murder of two people in Arkansas, and robbery and murder of two people in Georgia.

How the hell could such a smart, good-looking guy like him get into so much trouble? His daddy worked in construction, and for a while he'd worked with him. It didn't take long for Perry to realize that he didn't like working in the hot Alabama sun for minimum wage, not when he could sell drugs in an air conditioned bar while drinking a beer.

His parents, Wallace and Eulene, were religious and often held church meetings in their home. But Gene Perry had grander ideas and liked living in the fast lane, even though it had landed his ass in prison on several different occasions.

In preparing his defense, Perry got a haircut first thing, clipping off the dyed blond fuzz that had adorned his head during the summer of 1980. His natural hair color was dark brown, and it matched his mustache, which he was keeping because he thought it made him look handsome.

He knew he needed to change his appearance, so he lifted weights and dropped pounds as best he could in jail.

He was also busy writing down his alibi for the time he was supposed to have been in Van Buren, Arkansas. After all, it was Damon Peterson who robbed that store and killed those people. Not him, Gene Perry. He was visiting his parents, his ex-wife, and his daughters in Oxford, Alabama. They would vouch for him. They had already promised him they would. He'd also called in favors of friends who would testify that Gene Perry was merely the person who helped Damon Peterson fence the jewelry stolen in Arkansas.

Getting his ducks in a row took time, and he had plenty of that. He looked upon his alibi as a book he was writing, and as any good crime writer would, he had to provide details to fill out the puzzle of who he really was.

CHAPTER THIRTY

Bedazzled by the girl who wanted him to join her and others in the Canadian bush, Rick continually thought about a bank robbery as being a way to make the necessary money he'd need to join the girl and her group.

While he was living in Chinatown, north of downtown Vancouver, he purchased a pellet gun and began formulating his plan to rob a bank. With the encouragement of two cases of beer he'd stolen from a beer truck, he mapped out his plan with the skill and reasoning only an alcoholic understands.

On the morning of January 13th, 1981, Rick went to a used clothing store and bought a suit coat and pants. He pulled them over his ordinary work clothes, placed a pellet gun in a briefcase, and posed as a business man. In a tote bag he also bought at the store, he carried a hard hat. After robbing the bank, his plan was to discard the suit and don the hard hat, thus appearing to be a construction worker.

He walked to the Bank of Nova Scotia, the bank he planned to rob, but when he got there, a television news team was out in the street in front of the bank filming a story for the evening news. He waited until that was finished, never considering that a bank being filmed for the evening news might be a bad omen.

Instead, he flagged down a cab, tossed the hard hat in the backseat, and asked the cab driver to wait on him while he went into the bank to make a withdrawal.

He then walked into the bank and stood at one of the registers. When a woman asked if she could help him, he placed the briefcase on the counter and showed her the pellet gun, which looked like anything but a child's toy.

"Put the money in the briefcase," Rick told the woman.

She did, and so did the teller at the register next to her.

Rick walked out of the bank, found his waiting cab, and climbed inside to the front seat, next to the driver.

"Take me to New West Minister," he told him.

When they were halfway there, the cab driver suddenly pulled over and turned off the motor.

"What are you doing?" shouted Ricky.

The driver pointed to the rearview mirror that showed a police car behind him.

Rick reached across the man and opened his car door.

"You have to go."

The cabbie exited the vehicle, and Rick scooted over behind the wheel. Before he could start the car, it was surrounded by police, and they fired at the car, forcing Rick to raise his hands in surrender.

He exited the car and was immediately pounced upon by two German shepherds, who held him down by snarling and attacking him. Because Rick was dressed in two sets of clothes, the dogs didn't break the skin.

After he was taken to the police station, he was booked as Ivo Shapox because that was the name on the identification card he showed the police. Probably because he didn't look like a person whose last name would be Shapox, they held one of Rick's fingers under a microscope to see if it matched the print on the identification card.

"Who are you? You obviously aren't Ivo Shapox. In fact, I don't think you are even Canadian," an officer said.

Rick's suntan from his days on the Florida beach was still evident, and his accent didn't sound Canadian. But still he refused to tell his true name. They placed Rick in a cell next to a man who said he was getting out soon, and that he would help him with whatever he needed done on the outside. Not familiar with Canadian law, Rick didn't know how long he could be held, and he worried about his few possessions in his rented room. He chatted some more with his neighbor and decided he could trust the man.

"I'll give you my address, and if you will, you can go there and keep my stuff for me until I get out."

And after more conversation, Rick let down his guard. Perhaps he was exhausted from running, perhaps he just needed a friend, or perhaps he needed to get some things off his chest.

"I'm wanted in Arkansas for a jewelry store robbery. Two people were shot and killed."

Rick didn't know he was talking to an undercover policeman, who was in the jail in hopes of finding out information from a prisoner in the other cell next to him.

In a few days, Richard Phillip Anderson was being flown by commercial airlines to Fort Smith, Arkansas, where, dressed in slacks and a sports jacket, he was escorted off the plane. His wrists were handcuffed in front of him, and Sheriff Trellon Ball's arm was hooked inside Anderson's left elbow. Van Buren Assistant Police Chief Wayne Hicks, Detective Don Taylor of the Arkansas State Police, and Ron Fields accompanied them. The men were happy they didn't have to drive the 2,500 mile return trip from Vancouver to bring him home.

Florida had still not released Malantino/Peterson/Perry to Crawford County officials.

RICHARD ANDERSON, WITH PERM HE GOT IN CANADA
TO DISGUISE HIS APPEARANCE

CHAPTER THIRTY-ONE

Rick was locked up in a jail that had been labeled sub-standard in Van Buren, Arkansas. He was questioned on January 26th at 11:47 a.m. and asked to write down his statement. He told them about his first meeting with Damon Peterson.

> We were staying at some campground at Beaver Lake with a man by the name of Pete, who was with some red-haired girl. They were driving a red International Travelall. Everything was going good until we got into it because he called me pussy whipped. I was packing up to leave when the guy in the next space known as Damon invited us to camp with them. He said they had plenty of room. He was camped with a girl in a pop-up camper with a blue Cadillac. The next afternoon, he knew I was low on money, and he said he would cover our food. He said he had a scheme for making money and I might be interested, and hell, I fell for it hook, line, and sinker.

Two men were appointed his lawyers: Bill Cromwell and Sam Hugh Park. He was charged with capital murder.

Rick Anderson could tell by looking at Sam Hugh Park that he was gay. Anderson did not like gays or queers or fags or fairies—whatever the going term was. He discussed his aversion to homosexuals with Cromwell, who assured him that Park was a fine lawyer and that was the only criteria by which a lawyer should be judged.

Rick ran his hands through his long, curly, black hair. He'd gotten a permanent in Canada to help disguise himself.

"Okay, I guess it will be okay. If you say so."

He liked Cromwell immediately, and he guessed he'd have to trust him.

In addition to being charged with capital murder in Arkansas, Anderson discovered upon returning to the United States that he was also being charged with murder, along with Damon Peterson—alias Damon Malantino, alias Eugene Wallace Perry—in the murder of a woman and her son at a Georgia campground in late August of 1980, just weeks before the Arkansas robbery and murders. The bodies found in Georgia were tied with rope and executed by two bullets to the head in the same way that Kenneth Staton and Suzanne Ware were.

In the dank, cold cell, Rick Anderson recalled his Seventh Day Adventist religion and prayed that he could prove he was never in the state of Georgia, except in passing through when he and Damon and their women fled Arkansas bound for Atlanta to sell the stolen diamonds. He would plead innocent to the Staton murders. He tied Mr. Staton and his young daughter up, but Damon had fired the shots.

He'd had some frightening messages delivered to him in the Van Buren jail from Damon, who told him that he must not identify him as his partner. Damon said he had Mafia connections, and he knew the addresses of both Rick's parents in Florida and his sister in Topeka, Kansas, because he'd seen both of Anderson's drivers licenses issued from both states with the addresses of his folks and his sister with whom he'd lived at various times.

Rick truly believed that Damon could harm him or have him murdered. He was very convincing, and it was the convincing threats of harm to his family that partially kept Rick from escaping after the jewelry store robbery. He thought Damon's name should really be Demon.

Regardless of the threats, Rick wanted to turn over a new leaf. He didn't like who he'd become, and he was hoping for some salvation. Rick told Ron Fields everything: when he met Peterson on Beaver Lake, that they stayed at the Terry Motel, that they had met a woman at a Walmart parking lot the day before the robbery, that she had taken Peterson home with her to spend the night and returned him back the next morning, that they pawned a ring on the Wednesday morning in case they might need some cash, and that they sold the Cadillac and bought a Plymouth and fled to Atlanta to sell the jewelry after renting a storage unit for his motorcycle and Damon's pop-up camper. He gave Ron Fields the names of Chantina Ginn and Loralei Peterson, who could back up his story. He spilled his guts, leaving only a little bit out of his confession that did not relate to the Arkansas murders.

On a visit to a psychiatrist in Fort Smith for determination if Anderson was mentally fit to stand trial, Sam Hugh Park arranged for Debbye Hughes with the Fort Smith *Southwest Times Record* newspaper to interview him. Park wanted the newspaper readers to see a picture of a handsome young man who had fallen under the evil influence of a homicidal maniac.

"Poverty makes men do strange things they would not otherwise do," he whispered to the reporter before she began.

The exchange during the interview was as follows.

Reporter:	How do you keep your spirits up?
Anderson:	I try not to think about the ordeal I'm facing.
Reporter:	What are your hopes for the future?
Anderson:	I just want to get my life back together. I just try like hell to keep my spirits up.
Reporter:	If you are released, what will you do?

Anderson: I'll probably go back and live with my sister in Topeka.

Reporter: Did you kill Kenneth Staton and his daughter?

Anderson: No, I did not.

Debbye Hughes asked Anderson many questions that he did not answer because his attorney, Sam Hugh Park, signaled him not to. He did allow Anderson to tell the reporter about his Seventh Day Adventist family and how he had fallen out of the habit of attending church. He also explained that he married right out of high school, divorced, remarried again, and divorced again. He was clearly a young man who enjoyed the company of women but who had difficulty staying married. He also stated that drugs and alcohol had caused him to make many wrong decisions, for which he was now paying.

Sam Hugh Park was an excellent lawyer, but liquor and assignations with men of disreputable character had taken its toll. He'd lost a prestigious job as an Assistant U. S. Attorney and was now practicing out of his home in Van Buren. Perhaps Park thought this case would be his chance for redemption, and he could prove himself. He wanted to try the case in the newspapers. He wanted the readers to see how a handsome young man—the son of an IBM engineer, who had been raised in a Christian home—could fall in with a bad person and have his life ruined.

Park and Cromwell were succeeding in their plan to present the good side of Richard Anderson to the public by granting interviews to the media, and it worked perfectly until an order was issued by the Circuit Court of Crawford County in March of 1981:

> The defendant, Richard Anderson Perry, should be, and he is hereby, restrained and ordered by this court from granting any interviews or making any statements to the press, radio, television, or other members of the

news and television media until after the completion of the trial of the defendant Damon Peterson, a/k/a Damon Malantino, a/k/a Eugene Perry, which is set for trial on May 4, 1981.

That order foiled any other plans of Cromwell and Park for pretrial publicity, but they still had gotten the word out and ruffled the feathers of local law enforcement.

* * * * * *

Sam Hugh Park, a man in his late thirties, had no way of knowing that in four months his very own mother would be found dead in her home on top of Log Town Hill in Van Buren. And that he would be the only suspect the police would pursue.[1] Thus, while embroiled in a murder defense case that should have taken all his time and energy, he was also in the unenviable position of having to fend off the very prosecutors and law enforcement officers who were on the opposing side in the biggest criminal case of his young career. For a man trying to revive his career with his court-appointed defense of Anderson, his mother's death and the accusations that followed took their toll. He performed in the courtroom surprisingly well and passionately helped represent his client.

It would be his last hurrah.

---

[1] See best-selling true crime book *Blind Rage*, also by Anita Paddock, available at Amazon.com and elsewhere.

CHAPTER THIRTY-TWO

Where is Cindy Sue Brown? That's what everyone wanted to know. She wasn't the key witness, but she was definitely a witness that Georgia and Arkansas authorities wanted to find. She and Perry were a couple. She knew things about Perry that probably no one else knew.

Cindy had known that Perry had not been truthful with Anderson about the money they'd received from the sale of the stolen jewelry. Perry had held some jewelry back with one of his pals in Atlanta. When the time was right, he told Cindy, just the two of them would go back to Atlanta and finish the sale.

When Anderson and Perry were arrested by Jacksonville Beach police on the night of September 23rd, 1980, following the shootout at the motel and tavern, Cindy Sue Brown took off. A good bet was that she went to Atlanta and sold the rest of the jewelry to the fence who was holding it for their return.

Cindy had been Perry's girlfriend off and on for several years. Her grandmother lived in the same town in Alabama as Perry, and Cindy spent lots of time living with her grandmother.

Cindy and Perry were interested in the same thing: sex, drugs, and booze. She'd been smoking marijuana since she was thirteen and graduated to hard drugs. That those two would meet seemed almost like destiny.

But Cindy was afraid of Perry. He had once broken her ankle when she tried to leave him. When he had called her from a Florida prison and demanded she meet him at Camp Paradise in Tyrone, Georgia, she went.

Now she was nowhere to be found and wouldn't be for a couple of years, long after the trials of Perry and Anderson were concluded.

Eventually, Arkansas authorities would catch up with her. She had fled to Texas and then California, where she was arrested for prostitution. Georgia grabbed her and charged her as an accessory to the campground murders and imprisoned her on a lesser charge. After Georgia paroled her, she was arrested by Van Buren police and charged with conspiracy to commit robbery, a charge previously filed in 1983 in connection with the Staton robbery and murders.

During her six-month confinement in the Crawford County Jail and a hospital stay for an emergency hysterectomy, she became the recipient of prayers from a local group of ladies from Van Buren and Alma.

On Monday, February 11th, 1985, she apologized to the Staton family and pleaded no contest to the charges. She explained that all her trouble stemmed from her association with Perry and drugs. She told the court that both of her parents died violently: her mother by suicide, and her father by murder. She claimed she had been an honor student and president of her high school's student body.

She was transferred to the state women's prison in Pine Bluff, where she was soon paroled and never heard from again.

CHAPTER THIRTY-THREE

Damon Peterson (the name he was known by at that time by Arkansas officials) was returned to Arkansas to stand trial for murder on February 6th, 1981. He'd received ten years for the shootings in Jacksonville Beach.

Ron Fields had hoped Florida would allow the suspect to be tried first in Arkansas, and a "Demand for a Speedy Trial" had even been filed against the state of Arkansas by Eugene Wallace Perry/Malantino. Florida wanted him first though, so they kept him until they tried him.

The Georgia authorities would wait to try him after they saw what would happen to him in Arkansas.

Back on September 30th, 1980, Georgia investigators had questioned Eugene Wallace Perry (the name he was known by in Georgia) about the time he'd spent at Camper's Paradise in Tyrone, Georgia, from June 1980 to the end of August 1980. Perry said he'd lived there under the alias of Jim Jackson or Pop-Up Jim. He said he'd known Barbara Price and Allen Price very well, and that Barbara Price knew he was using an alias, and that they often smoked marijuana together. He said he left the campgrounds on August 23rd, 1980, just a few days before she and her son were killed, and that he was horrified to think that anyone could possibly accuse him of killing Barbara and her son. He also told the Georgia authorities that Richard Anderson was not in Georgia at the campgrounds, and he hadn't met him until much later.

Upon arrival by car driven by Sheriff Ball and Wayne Hicks of the Van Buren Police Department, Peterson/Perry was ushered into the Crawford County Courthouse holding cells where he was fingerprinted, photographed, and strip searched. There were no tattoos to be seen.

They then went to the sheriff's office to wait for Ron Fields to interview Peterson/Perry and possibly get a statement. It was a twelve-hour drive from Florida, and Ball and Hicks were tired and ready to go home and get some sleep.

When Ron Fields arrived, they were both sitting down with the suspect, drinking coffee. Fields was surprised at Peterson/Perry's change of appearance since he'd seen him last in September. He wore a red plaid shirt, and his hair was short and dark and straight and parted on the side. He looked like a school teacher or maybe a hardware clerk.

Fields and Peterson/Perry exchanged greetings.

"They haven't appointed you an attorney yet. I suspect it will be two, but that's up to the court."

"Have you talked to my attorney in Florida?"

"Kaylor? The public defender?"

"Yes," Fields said. "He was most interested in our case here in Arkansas. I entered a plea down there. I wasn't the one who shot up the tavern so those charges of attempted murder were dropped. Course what I was hoping for was federal time."

"I hear life is easier in federal prison. By the way," Fields asked, "what name do we call you?" He paused a moment. "You were first charged in Jacksonville Beach as Malantino. Damon Malantino. What about Damon Peterson?"

"Call me Gene Perry, but you might just say aka/Damon Peterson or aka/Damon Malantino. I understand there's been some serious implications against me."

"Yes," Fields said and handed a shorter version of Anderson's statement to Perry to read.

Perry read the statement, mouthing the words as he read.

Fields gave him a few minutes.

"Now, if you'd like to say anything, like to give your side of the story, you can put everything in your statement. I must tell you that Anderson made a very good appearance on TV yesterday. He's a baby-faced, easy-go-lucky guy that was dominated by an evil personality, according to him. Anderson said you bought guns and silencers, spent money on high-class hotels. Your name is on everything—Damon Peterson, that is."

"But the basic thing remains is that he's lying. But I'm not him—Damon Peterson—you see. I'm Gene Perry."

"If you want to make a statement, then do so, and we'll check it out just like we did Anderson's. He told us he met you at a campground, robbed the jewelry store in Van Buren, and fled to Atlanta, where you fenced the diamonds. Everything he said checks out. Only he says you murdered the Statons. He just tied them up."

Perry tossed the statement on the desk like it was yesterday's newspaper.

"I don't want to be electrocuted. I don't even want to get life in prison without parole. Not for this. I don't want to implicate myself in any kind of way or in any way that if I was—I'm not saying I was—if I was connected in any kind of way, but I don't want to implicate myself in any way at this time."

Fields nodded. "I understand that, but what I'm saying—"

Perry interrupted Fields with, "He may be putting me here and there, and there may be ten thousand eye witnesses, but the fact remains about that jewelry store thing."

Fields continued to listen, encouraging Perry to keep talking.

"Tell your side, so we can check it out."

"Now, I'm the type that needs all the help I can get. I could tell the truth, but it might be damaging to me. That's why I'm waiting on my lawyers."

"We've got the blue and white Cadillac, the pop-up camper, and the Plymouth you traded the Cadillac for. We've got the Horseshoe Bend registration at Beaver Lake. So many things with Damon's name on them."

Perry shifted around in his chair. "Goddamn! Maybe I'm guilty of camping out somewhere, but that don't make me a jewelry store robber."

Ball and Fields looked at each other. Their facial expressions didn't change, but somehow a mental message passed between them. *We got him.* Perry didn't realize it, but he'd just placed himself in a most perilous position.

"Well," said Fields, "do you want to tell us what all you did those days at Beaver Lake?"

"When can you appoint me an attorney?"

"As I've said, I can't appoint you one. I'll tell the judge that you need one, and he can take it from there."

"That's right. There's so much here, and it does involve my life. I may be making the biggest mistake of my life by not laying it right on the table here and now."

Fields motioned to Sheriff Ball. "Are you ready to take him up to his cell?"

Sheriff Ball gave a conspiratorial hint of a smile and said, "Sure thing, sir."

Perry and Anderson would be spending the night in jail under the same roof, under the same scattered nighttime clouds, under the same fingernail moon that hung over the Van Buren homes of Kenneth Staton and Suzanne Ware. It cast only a sliver of light now, but by and by, it would become a full moon triumphantly hanging over the town.

If Ruth Staton slept a little sounder that night, or perhaps more peacefully, no one will ever know for sure, but one man, Ron Fields, hoped that she did.

Eugene Wallace Perry
... first to be convicted

EUGENE WALLACE PERRY, AFTER ARREST FOR MURDERS

PERRY WITH CIGAR IN TOUGH GUY WALK

CHAPTER THIRTY-FOUR

Even the newspapers couldn't get Perry's name correct because the headlines on Saturday, February 7th, 1981, of the *Southwest Times Record* read, "Suspect Returned: Peterson's hearing to be next week."

Perry (finally under his official name as determined by his birth certificate) was moved to the Sebastian County Jail by Sheriff Bill Cauthron to a maximum-security cell. He had two attorneys appointed to represent him against a charge of capital murder: Ron Harrison and Steve Sharum, men who both lived in Fort Smith.

They immediately set a plan in motion to change the venue for the court trials—that their client couldn't get a fair trial in the Crawford County Courthouse in Van Buren because of the publicity surrounding the murders on September 10th, 1980. Eventually the venue was changed to the Sebastian County Courthouse in Fort Smith, just across the river from Van Buren. There were plenty of scoffs made about that "change of venue," including petitions signed by lawyers and laymen alike who disagreed with the decision. Alas, the petitions failed, and Judge David Partain of the Twelfth Judicial Circuit set the trial dates for both men in mid-March.

But when a star witness, Chantina Ginn, Rick Anderson's girl friend, who could account for his first time ever meeting with Perry at Beaver

Lake, was unable to travel due to a serious motorcycle accident, the case was postponed. The prosecuting attorney's office received the report from Chantina's doctor, Doctor David E. Thurman at the Orthopedic Clinic of Topeka, stating she was in a serious motorcycle accident on April 19th, 1981, in which she sustained a severe open injury above the left knee with fracturing and loss of bone, both of the end of the femur and upper tibia. She underwent prolonged surgery the day of the admission for repair and subsequently had been confined to the hospital. He estimated she would be in a cast for the next two to three months and would require skin and wound care.

Judge David Partain granted a postponement and scheduled July 23rd, 1981, to be the trial date. He quietly pondered on this case that was full of tragedy. A young girl just out of high school jumps on the back of a motorcycle with a handsome young man and ends up being a star witness in two capital murder trials. And once again, she jumps on the back of a motorcycle and ends up seriously wounded.

The thrill of a ride on a motorcycle with a good-looking man was not worth the risk.

From pretrial depositions, both sides knew that Chantina would testify that she had met Anderson in Topeka, Kansas, and that they had traveled by motorcycle to camp out at Beaver Lake in Arkansas, and that, there, they met Damon Peterson and Loralei Peterson for the first time. She would also testify that Anderson and Peterson returned to their camp after a short trip with two orange nylon bags full of jewelry, and that the four of them traveled to Atlanta and then to Florida. Her testimony was crucially important to Ron Fields's case against Perry, as well as to Anderson, who was going to have to face a Georgia murder charge after the Staton trial.

CHAPTER THIRTY-FIVE

Opening arguments began after a jury was chosen that included Dennis Meeks, Norma Hale, Judith Willcoxon, Judith Hogan, Rubin E. Jester, Alva Harman, Linda Kennon, Carmelita Harrison, Robert Heinold, Mary June Moore, Theodore Applegate, and Lawrence E. Sharum, Jr. (no relation to the defendant's attorney, Steve Sharum).

Eugene Wallace Perry, clad in a dark suit provided by the county, was seated at the defense table across a wide space from where the prosecutors sat at a similar table. Each of the tables was mahogany, well-worn, and situated in front of the raised mahogany paneled bench where the judge sat.

The long, darkly paneled courtroom was about half full, and the spectators were separated from where the lawyers and judge sat by a mahogany fence and gate. It was obvious that the architect and the carpenters had used care and pride in the building of that courtroom.

The security people stood up front, and both Sheriff Trellon Ball and Sheriff Bill Cauthron stood silently at the back of the room. There had been rumors that the Mafia would try to help Perry escape.

Janet traveled from Paris, Texas, to attend the trial. Since she would not be testifying, she was allowed to be in the courtroom. The other members of the family—Ruth, Karen, and Elaine—waited in the hallway for when each would be called to testify. The benches they sat on had clearly been there for a long time since initials and dates and names had been carved into the wood by anxious or angry people that didn't know any better. Or perhaps they did, and carving graffiti on the benches was a way to thumb their noses at the court system.

The Staton women were prepared mentally and emotionally to testify. All three would say what needed to be said, nothing more. If they were frightened to sit in the same room with the man who killed Kenneth and Suzanne, they surely would not let him know it. For the past ten months, they'd been in survival mode, not allowing themselves to break down. The word "stoic" had been created with them in mind.

By the time Ron Fields spoke to the jury, he knew the case inside and out. He had such sympathy and admiration for the Staton family that he had become quite passionate about the case. He wanted to do his very best to see that Perry got the death sentence for his crimes. He was certain Perry was a cold-blooded killer who had shown no remorse or compassion.

Ron Fields, dressed in a navy suit, starched white shirt, and maroon tie, began his opening by looking directly at the jury with a look of high regard for their position. His demeanor was serious, but not autocratic or boastful, as if he was the most intelligent man in the room. He appeared sincere in his representation of the two people who couldn't speak for themselves: a daddy and his youngest daughter.

Ron Fields began: "Now this case actually starts prior to September 10th, 1980, when two people get together up at Rogers, Arkansas, to decide that they are going to rob a jewelry store located in the Cloverleaf Plaza in Van Buren on the Wednesday, the 10th of September. Those people are known to us as a man named Damon Peterson, who uses some other names also, and Richard Phillip Anderson. Now they plan out this robbery, and they take along some rope and gags, and they plan things by surveillance of the store around closing time so everything goes like clockwork. They enter the store while the owner, Kenneth Staton, and his daughter, Suzanne Ware, are preparing to close the store in their usual way by counting the cash register and emptying the jewelry cases and placing them in the safes in the back room.

"Two men enter, tie them up securely with ropes and gags, and proceed to steal the most expensive items in the store—worth close to one hundred thousand dollars. They are careful not to leave fingerprints or hit any alarms. After grabbing the jewelry, they shoot both victims twice in the head at close range. They do this so there will be no witnesses. Then they steal Suzanne's jeep, drive across the street to the Safeway parking lot, where one gets out and gets on a Harley-Davidson, and they travel to a local apartment complex and leave the jeep and go back to the Terry Motel across the bridge in Fort Smith, where they've been staying. They pack up their stuff, along with the loot they've stolen and placed in orange nylon bags, and head back to Rogers."

Judge David Partain—a tall, lanky man with blond hair that was graying—was known for fairness and a keen legal mind. He was very judicial in his posture, sitting at his desk flanked by two flags representing Arkansas and the United States. The jury listened intently. Eugene Wallace Perry didn't look up but sat, drawing pictures on a legal pad.

George Fowler, a man who worked at Hunt's Department Store next door to the jewelry store, was called first. He described how Elaine Barham and Karen Staton had come to his store to ask if he had seen their dad and sister. He'd gone with them to the jewelry store next door and was able to jiggle open the front door.

Elaine Barham testified that she had found her father and sister lying on their stomachs with gags in their mouths, and their hands and feet were tied with rope. She had tried to cut the ropes off their hands and tried to take the gags out of their mouths, hoping they were still alive.

"It was when I was trying to help Daddy get the gag out of his mouth that the police arrived, and they made me leave."

Fields excused the witness. The lawyers for the defense had no questions. Seeing that some members of the jury were clearly upset by Elaine's testimony, Judge Partain announced that everyone would take a thirty-minute recess.

Judge Partain went back to his chambers. He prayed that his daughter, Paige, would never have to go through anything as horrible as Mr. Staton's daughters, Suzanne or Elaine, had to endure. He'd already been told in the pretrial hearings that Richard Anderson would testify that Mr. Staton was shot first, and that the medical examiner had theorized that Mr. Staton had gripped his teeth when he was shot, and that was why Elaine had been unable to remove his gag. But Suzanne had probably fainted before she died and, therefore, her gag was easily pulled from her mouth.

CHAPTER THIRTY-SIX

The next witness called was Don Taylor, the investigator with the Arkansas State Police, who had worked the case with the doggedness every good detective possesses. He had been with the state police for twenty-one years and investigated major crimes in Crawford, Sebastian, and Franklin Counties.

He described the scene he found at the Staton Jewelry Store and explained that one of his first jobs was to take crime scene photographs, which were entered as exhibits. The attorneys for Perry objected to many of the photos, and Judge Partain ruled that, in order not to inflame the jurors, only a few pictures that were less gory and less bloody would be allowed.

The trial continued with Taylor's testimony of finding four .22 caliber bullet casings at the scene, a root beer can, and a Dr. Pepper can left on the counter, which were dusted for prints, but they came out incomplete. He led the jury with him to the Terry Motel, Horseshoe Bend on Beaver Lake, a used car lot, a storage unit that held a pop-up camper and a Harley-Davidson motorcycle, and the evidence inside the camper that implicated Eugene Wallace Perry with the robberies and murders.

The residents of Crawford County counted on the editor of their newspaper, *The Press Argus*, to give them the more personal and human side of the trial. Garrick Feldman, a talented editor of his column, "The Publisher's Notebook," told his readers of one woman whom Ron Fields called to testify.

He wrote: "Fields calls a young girl, and she starts saying how one day last September she was leaving Walmart when she noticed a couple of men, and hardly anybody's prepared for what she has to tell the court. Her name is Pat Etier, and she is slim and blonde, and if you don't know why she's here you might think she's going to say she remembered seeing Perry walking around Cloverleaf Plaza with his friend Anderson, and that's about it. But as her tale unfolds, you soon realize she's the most dramatic witness yet. She's soft-spoken, and you might think she's shy, but it's more than that: she's afraid because what she has to say could put Perry in the electric chair if the jury believes her.

"Pat Etier's story is that she got picked up by Perry and Anderson the day before the murders, and they went to the Terry Motel after they bought a couple of packs of beer. She says the room was in the back, and once inside, they drank the beer, and the younger of the two showed her his tattoo. He said his name was Rick, and the older one said his name was Damon. He said they were passing hot checks. She left a couple of hours later but returned to take Perry home with her where she lives in Graphic with her young son.

"Although she appears calm as she tells her story, she's scared because she might be in danger for agreeing to testify in court. Months ago she had come forward and told the authorities what she knew, and you can't help admiring her for that. There are rumors that Perry has bragged about his Mafia connections, and let's face it, anyone who says he's in the Mafia probably wouldn't be accepted into that elite organization.

"But still, it's never easy to give testimony that might send someone to an electric chair. Family and friends may not look too kindly at that, and Mrs. Etier may have thought about that a lot, but she's spoken out anyway. The young woman may have her weaknesses, but if she's telling the truth, you have to say she has a conscience."

Feldman's readers nodded their heads, pursed their lips, and uttered an "Ah-hah, so that's the way they found out who did it. What if she'd never come forward?"

What Feldman didn't know, or didn't report, was that during the earlier months of pretrial discovery, Perry's lawyers had conducted their depositions of the witnesses against Perry. They told Perry that Pat Etier would be called to testify against him, and once again, he'd set his mind to work and hatched a way to get Pat Etier to change her story.

Perry requested permission to write Pat Etier a letter. He begged her to come and visit him in jail to see if, up close and personal, she could really say for sure that he was the man who spent the night with her.

He wrote on Sunday, July 5th, 1981, from the Sebastian county jail:

Dear Mrs. Etier,

I'm writing to you from the bottom of my heart, and I hope and pray that you do not misunderstand why I am writing. It is certainly not my intention to frighten you in any way. For several months I have contemplated as to whether I should or I should not write to you. I was afraid that I would upset you, but you will see that is not by any means my purpose or intent of this letter, in fact, it's quite the contrary. I am writing to ask a favor of you, which would mean everything to me, and I will ask that shortly, but first, maybe you are asking yourself "Why me? Why write to me?" So if you will give me a few minutes of your time, I would be forever grateful to you, and not only me, but I have a family, 2 daughters, one 17 yrs old and one 15, and I'm certain they would appreciate this request also . . . .

You are the only witness who would be able to give a most accurate description of Damon, and if your description is accurate, as I'm sure it must be, then it would be quite impossible for me, Eugene Wallace Perry, to be Damon Peterson . . . .

Please come talk to me, look at me, compare me, whatever you need to do, but please, in your own heart and mind, don't make a mistake that could cost an innocent man his life.

When Pat Etier got the letter, she read it over and over. Even though he wrote that it was not a threat, she knew that it really was. Pat was anything but naïve, and she firmly believed that, if there had been a gun in her home in Graphic, Perry would have used it to kill her and her little boy.

Pat had not always been the most virtuous girl around, and she had hung out with some rough characters, but she had a conscience, and she was going to let it be her guide. She, by God, would testify at that trial and tell the truth, and she was not going to be intimidated by a man who told her his name was Damon and that he'd like to teach her little boy how to shoot a gun. And so she didn't let Perry scare her, even though he had done some really, really scary things.

Following Pat Etier, Fields called Ruth Staton and then Karen Staton to the stand. Ruth Staton testified that she recognized Perry as the man who came into their jewelry store with his wife looking for a wedding set during the first days of September.

She and her daughter Karen also identified jewelry found on Perry, as well as that in his motel room, that was part of their inventory. Even the wedding ring Mrs. Staton had given her husband for their twenty-fifth wedding anniversary, the ring he always wore, was found on Perry's finger the day he was arrested in Florida.

When the court recessed for the weekend, Eugene Wallace Perry sat down in his cell room and went over his defense with a calendar in front of him. His defense was that he was never in Arkansas in his life, that he was in Alabama visiting his family and buying school clothes for his daughter during the early days of September, and, most importantly, Damon Peterson was somebody else. Perry said the only connections he had with Peterson and Anderson was that he acted as their fence when they came to him in Atlanta asking him to get rid of the jewelry.

CHAPTER THIRTY-SEVEN

The Perry defense team of Ron Harrison and Steve Sharum began their case when Perry's daughters, Tonya and Dawn, testified that their father took them shopping for school clothes at The Red Hanger Shop at a mall in Oxford, Alabama, on September 9th, 1980. His mother and father, Eulene and Wallace, claimed he arrived at their home in Oxford around ten at night on September 11th and spent the night with them. His ex-wife, Glenda, testified that she visited with him off and on during those days in September.

Eugene Wallace Perry did not testify in his defense.

The jury deliberated two hours and returned a guilty verdict. After an additional two hours and fifteen minutes, they read their verdict: Wallace Eugene Perry would die for his crime.

Perry muttered over and over that he was innocent, and he was obviously shaken by the decision.

Judge Partain said, "It now becomes my painful duty to sentence you to death by electrocution." He then set the date for March 22nd, 1982, some eight months away.

When asked if he wanted to address the court, Perry responded, "Well, I'm not guilty, for one thing, and I'm not Damon Peterson, for another."

Those words spoken by Perry were the first the Staton family had heard at the trial. Karen was shocked by his deep Southern accent. Even though she lived in Arkansas, a state considered part of the South, she had never before heard an accent that thickly Southern—with Rs missing and syllables drawn out from two or three to four or five.

The Staton family sat in the courtroom with their typical stoic demeanor. They amazed their friends by not crying when the verdict was read. Or shouting with joy that Perry would be electrocuted. They took it in stride, just like they had done in everything else prior to the verdict.

Janet returned to Texas, with a promise that she would be back for Anderson's trial.

Karen was back living in her home she had bought prior to the robbery. She worked at nights and on the weekends stripping wallpaper and scraping paint that had been applied to lovely hardwood doors and cornices in the house. Her kitchen now had a new refrigerator and stove, and its floors were recovered with almond-colored linoleum. She once briefly thought she'd have her family over for dinner, but she quickly remembered what had happened the last time she cooked for her family.

The store was entering its busiest season, and salesmen were calling and Christmas items were arriving daily. Karen told friends who asked how she felt about the verdict: "Right now I'm relieved it's over. We've got Christmas coming up, and that's all I can think about right now."

Elaine didn't like showing her feelings to the world. She, after all, had a rambunctious toddler who occupied her days. Once Ben was put to bed, she slept on the couch with the light on until her husband came home from work. Only then did she feel safe, and she would turn off the light and climb into bed with her husband. That would not change, no matter what happened to Perry and Anderson.

Ruth Staton felt more emotion, but she, too, kept it hidden and stored deep in her heart. She had two dear friends she often visited after work. One was Linda Patton, who was also a young widow and was raising two young girls on her own. They often ate their evening meal together in Linda's kitchen.

The other was her neighbor, Evelyn Hess. They'd sit in the living room and watch television until Ruth would announce it was her bedtime and time to go home. She had over 200 sympathy cards, mostly still unread, that she kept in a box in her bedroom. Perhaps, one day, she thought, she'd be able to read them. Not now. Not now.

CHAPTER THIRTY-EIGHT

A hint of fall weather ushered in October 6th, 1981, the day that Richard Phillip Anderson was brought to the Sebastian County Courthouse where his trial for capital murder would begin.

Instead of looking like a man on the run in Canada, as he did when first brought to Van Buren, he was pale from spending almost ten months locked up in a cell.

Back in the winter, after he was first brought to Van Buren, Anderson had requested an interview with Garrick Feldman, the editor of the newspaper, who he'd figured out was a man of importance. If he could tell his story to the editor, and if the editor wrote a favorable column about him, that might help when he went on trial.

Instead, Feldman wrote:

> He says sometimes he's scared and hints he's afraid of what Perry might do to him. He rubs his scars on his temples and cracks his knuckles. Anderson is good at one thing: he's eager to evoke sympathy. He wants to be liked. He wants to be seen as a good guy who may have made a mistake or two. He gives you the impression

he thinks he's okay. Only he doesn't convince everyone of that. Far from it. His family background of upper-middle class—with a father an executive at a big corporation and a stay-at-home mom—makes him seem like a guy who wouldn't end up in Crawford County charged with capital murder. How did he get to where he was now?

The article didn't turn out the way Rick hoped it would, and he realized that this Feldman guy was smart and talented and not a country bumpkin who ran a little local newspaper.

He deeply regretted the hell he was putting his parents and siblings through, and he felt great sympathy for the Staton family. He would admit he was at the jewelry store and that he carried a gun and that he tied Kenneth and Suzanne up with ropes. But it was Perry who shot them.

It was a new trial, with a new jury, but much of the preliminary testimonies from witnesses were the same as they had been in the Perry trial. The police from Vancouver testified about arresting a man who claimed to be Ivo Shapox for attempting to rob a bank, then finding out that his real name was Richard Phillip Anderson. Anderson had befriended another inmate in a cell next to him and told him about how he had been hiding out in Canada for the past three months and that he and another man had robbed a jewelry store in a little town in Arkansas, and that the other man had murdered a crippled man and his young daughter so there would be no witnesses. The next-door cellmate turned out to be a detective with the Vancouver police.

The difference in the Anderson trial from the Perry trial was that the defendant took the stand.

After Anderson was sworn in, Bill Cromwell, the attorney for the defense, asked Anderson the usual obligatory questions of his early years. He led Anderson through the history of his coming to Beaver Lake, meeting Damon Peterson, as he was known then by Anderson, and leaving their campsite on Anderson's motorcycle to go to Van Buren to commit a robbery, either a jewelry store or a drug store, in Cloverleaf Plaza. That they decided on the jewelry store because it was easier to fence the stolen goods, and that, from casing the store for several days, it was determined that the robbery would take place on Wednesday, September 10th, at closing time.

Cromwell:	Where did you park?
Anderson:	Across the street at a grocery store parking lot.
Cromwell:	Do you remember the name of the grocery store?
Anderson:	I think it was a Safeway, but I don't know.
Cromwell:	What did you do after you parked there?
Anderson:	Okay, we walked over to the store.
Cromwell:	Okay, did Mr. Perry, or Peterson, whatever you want to call him, did he have any items of apparel to conceal his true identity?
Anderson:	Yes, sir. He was wearing a wig.
Cromwell:	Were you wearing a mask or anything to conceal your identity?
Anderson:	No, sir.
Cromwell:	Who entered the store first?
Anderson:	I did.
Cromwell:	Why did you go in first?
Anderson:	Because Damon instructed me to.
Cromwell:	What were you supposed to do when you got in the store?
Anderson:	Sit down and look at some jewelry.
Cromwell:	Why were you supposed to do that, and if so, who told you to do so?

Anderson: Okay, would you repeat the question?

Cromwell: Okay, you told us you went in the store first, you did it because he told you to, and you have told us what you were supposed to do was look at some jewelry. Is that right?

Anderson: That's right.

Cromwell: Who told you to do that, if anyone?

Anderson: Damon.

Cromwell: Did he tell you why you were supposed to do that?

Anderson: Okay, to get the attention of the fellow, you know, out of the back room.

Cromwell: Did you have a firearm in your possession?

Anderson: Yes, sir. I had a .38 caliber pistol.

Cromwell: Where did you get this .38 caliber pistol?

Anderson: From Damon.

Cromwell: Was it loaded?

Anderson: Yes, sir.

Cromwell: Had you ever fired it prior to entering the store?

Anderson: No, sir.

Cromwell: Did you fire it while you were in the jewelry store?

Anderson: No, sir.

Cromwell: As I understand it from the state's testimony, these two people were tied up?

Anderson: Yes, sir.

Cromwell: So that means some rope was taken into the jewelry store.

Anderson: Yes, sir.

153

Cromwell: Tell the jury who took the rope into the jewelry store?

Anderson: Damon.

Cromwell: What was that rope used for?

Anderson: To tie them up.

Cromwell: Tell the jury who actually tied these two people up.

Anderson: I did.

Cromwell: Why did you tie them up?

Anderson: Because Damon instructed me to.

Cromwell: What was your purpose in tying them up?

Anderson: Just so they couldn't get at any alarms or use the phone to call the authorities, you know, give us a chance to get away.

Cromwell: Okay, when you entered the jewelry store, did you have any idea at all that anyone was going to be killed?

Anderson: No, sir.

Cromwell: Did you kill Kenneth Staton?

Anderson: No, sir.

Cromwell: Did you kill Suzanne Ware?

Anderson: No, sir.

Cromwell: Did you tie them up so that Damon Peterson could kill them?

Anderson: No, sir.

Cromwell: Tell the jury again why you tied these two people up.

Anderson: Well, I tied them up just to give us a head start.

Cromwell: Okay, tell the jury so they can understand what other precautions Damon told you to take so that the

	alarms would not be set off? What other things did you do besides tie up Suzanne and Mr. Staton?
Anderson:	Well, he just instructed me to keep them away from any possible alarms or the telephone. He didn't want the cash registers touched at all. The money that was taken out of the store, they had already closed up the registers, and he had that on the back counter.
Cromwell:	Where did you learn how to tie up two people so they could not get free?
Anderson:	Damon instructed me.
Cromwell:	Where was this?
Anderson:	Damon, well, he told me a little bit over at the motel room.
Cromwell:	Terry Motel?
Anderson:	Yeah. And then as I was tying them up.
Cromwell:	Who showed you how to make the gags?
Anderson:	Damon made the gags.
Cromwell:	Where did he make them?
Anderson:	At the motel room.
Cromwell:	What material were the gags made from?
Anderson:	I think a washcloth.
Cromwell:	One that he got from the Terry Motel?
Anderson:	Yes.
Cromwell:	What kind of gun did Damon Peterson have in his possession?
Anderson:	He had a .22 pistol.
Cromwell:	Okay, did that pistol have any equipment on it.

Anderson: It had a big, long thing on it, on the end of it.

Cromwell: What is that?

Anderson: I guess it is a silencer.

Cromwell: Did you have any special equipment on the gun you were carrying?

Anderson: No, sir.

Cromwell: How long was it after you entered the store that Mr. Peterson came into the store?

Anderson: Oh, about a minute.

Cromwell: Okay. Who drew their gun first?

Anderson: I drew the gun first.

Cromwell: Who did you draw it on?

Anderson: Okay, Mr. Staton.

Cromwell: Why did you draw your gun first? What was the sequence of events?

Anderson: Okay, because the awkwardness of his gun, which he was carrying in a Walmart bag, it was decided that I would draw my gun first because it was smaller and would be easier to get out.

Cromwell: Who decided that?

Anderson: Damon.

Cromwell: What did you do then?

Anderson: We led them back to the back room.

Cromwell: Then what happened?

Anderson: Well, I tied them up.

Cromwell: Okay, after you tied up Mr. Staton and Suzanne, what happened next?

Anderson: Okay, we got the jewelry out of the front part of the store and brought it back to the back room and started going through things in the back.

Cromwell: What types of containers did you have to take the jewelry away from the store?

Anderson: They were nylon-type bags.

Cromwell: Where did they come from?

Anderson: Damon had them.

Cromwell: Did you then proceed to rob and pilfer the merchandise?

Anderson: Will you repeat that?

Cromwell: Did you take the merchandise from Staton's Jewelry?

Anderson: Yes, sir. We put it inside the bags.

Cromwell: How long did it take you to gather up the merchandise?

Anderson: I really wasn't keeping track of the time.

Cromwell: Did you have your gun with you?

Anderson: Okay, when Damon told me to tie them up, I laid my gun down on the counter.

Cromwell: Did either Mr. Staton or Suzanne resist?

Anderson: No, they were very cooperative.

Cromwell: What are your feelings about their deaths?

Anderson: It shouldn't have happened. I feel real bad about their deaths.

Cromwell: Did you kill either one of these people?

Anderson: No, sir.

Cromwell: Did you know they were going to be killed when they were?

Anderson: No, sir.

Cromwell: Did you assist in going through the safe in the back room?

Anderson: I was over by one of the safes, and I guess Damon had already been through it. I was over there just re-checking when he started shooting.

Cromwell: What did you do when you heard the first shot?

Anderson: I stood up, and I turned around, and it just startled me. I said, "What the hell are you doing?"

Cromwell: Did he respond?

Anderson: He said he didn't want any witnesses.

CHAPTER THIRTY-NINE

The questions continued until Cromwell stopped his examination and Ron Fields took over.

Fields: You said a minute ago, you were going through the safe when you heard the first shot?

Anderson: Yes.

Fields: Who was shot first?

Anderson: Mr. Staton.

Fields: Let's talk again about when you went into the store, and you went first?

Anderson: Yes.

Fields: And Mr. Staton waited on you. Did you view him as a threat?

Anderson: No, sir.

Fields: What about the girl?

Anderson: No, sir.

Fields: How tall was she?

Anderson: I am not sure.

Fields: Well, was she short, medium, tall?

Anderson: Sir, I really don't remember. A lot has happened.

Fields: Let me refresh your memory. Suzanne was five feet one inch, and Kenneth Staton was five feet three inches. How tall are you?

Anderson: Five nine.

Fields: How much do you weight?

Anderson: I don't know, sir.

Fields: How tall was Perry?

Anderson: I believe he's over six feet.

Fields: Okay, so to control these people, you tied them up.

Anderson: Yes, sir.

Fields: Tell us how you tied them up?

Anderson: Sir, I think that was all gone into before.

Fields: Why don't you tell us again?

Anderson: Well, we tied their hands and feet.

Fields: It wasn't just simply tying their hands and feet.

Anderson: It was their hands and feet tied behind their backs.

Fields: And were their hands and feet tied together?

Anderson: Yes.

Fields: What about the gags?

Anderson: He instructed me to put the gags in their mouths and then take a piece of rope and tie it to make sure the gags stayed there.

Fields: What did you tell these people while this was going on?

Anderson: Perry told them there wasn't nothing for them to worry about.

Fields: What did you say?

Anderson: I didn't tell them nothing.

Fields: You didn't tell them not to be afraid?

Anderson: Man, I was a nervous wreck myself being in there in the first place.

Fields: And Mr. Staton was shot first. What steps did you take to save Suzanne Ware?

Anderson: I didn't, sir. I was afraid for my own life.

Fields: From who?

Anderson: From Perry. I was unarmed at the time, and seeing what he was capable of doing at that time, sir.

And later, after more questioning, Judge Partain called for a ten-minute recess in order to give the jury a chance to go to the bathroom or get a drink of water. From experience as an attorney and a judge, he knew that jurors could hear just so much testimony before their minds would wander.

When the jury returned, Ron Fields proceeded to a different subject.

Fields: All right, Mr. Anderson, when you were inside the jewelry store, did you take anything other than the merchandise in the store counters and in the safe?

Anderson: Other than the merchandise?

Fields: Did you take any personal property off the victims?

Anderson: Yes. Damon told me to take the jewelry off the Sta tons. He said, he asked them to take off their jewelry, and they handed it to me.

Fields: Who handed it to you?

Anderson: Mr. Staton.

Fields: So it was before you tied him up?

Anderson: Yes.

Fields: What about his wallet?

Anderson: He handed that over.

Fields: They did everything they could to keep from getting hurt, didn't they?

Anderson: Yes, sir, they did, and they should not have been hurt.

Fields: That's what you thought when you walked in there with a loaded gun?

Anderson: Nobody was to get hurt, sir.

Fields: Somebody did get hurt, though, didn't they?

Anderson: Unfortunately, yes, sir.

Fields: Only two people walked out of that store, and you stayed with that other person after that and made no attempt to leave?

Anderson: I didn't think I had a choice, sir.

And with that last answer, Ron Fields announced to the judge and the jury and to Anderson that he had no other questions.

CHAPTER FORTY

On Wednesday, October 14th, 1981, after deliberating ten hours, the jury rendered its verdict: guilty on the charge of first degree murder, which carried with it a sentence of life in prison and a $15,000 fine. It was the verdict that Anderson's lawyers had hoped for.

Sam Hugh Park had asked in his summation: "Where is the evidence that he shot anybody? On the facts of the law, you must return a verdict of not guilty as to capital murder and guilty to first degree murder."

After the verdict was read, Rick Anderson's father, William Anderson, said, "We're just overjoyed. We expected the worst and got the best."

His father, following an early retirement, moved his family to Rogers in order to be closer to his son in prison in Arkansas. Ironically, he bought a little shop called Lost Treasures Flea Market and was bludgeoned to death with a hammer during a robbery in October of 1991. Ryan Baker, a twenty-year-old on parole from a previous sentence of robbery, was arrested for the murder. A customer reported seeing Baker and another man looking at a calculator.

Rick Anderson praised his legal team—Bill Cromwell and Sam Hugh Park—and thanked the judge and jury for their fair and impartial diligence in granting him his life.

* * * * * *

Anderson was transported back to Crawford County jail in a downpour, the kind of torrential rain that happens in the fall. Mother Nature's way of preparing her earth for the coming winter. Pictures appeared the next day in local papers of him sitting in the backseat of a police car, the windows streaked with rainfall that partially obscured the twenty-four-year-old from vision. What he was thinking, no one knew, but a good bet was that he was remembering the life he could have had and the one he was facing in the Arkansas penal system.

He later wrote a letter of apology to the Staton family. But it was too soon for the Statons to respond with anything but indignation, and they asked that he not contact them again. Anderson was a model prisoner and eventually taught himself both Greek and Hebrew so that he could make an educated decision on the faith he would eventually call his. Unlike the rest of his family, who were Seventh Day Adventist, he became a Messianic Jew, the religion he practices to this day. He asked for clemency from four different Arkansas governors, but he was refused every time.

He currently resides in a Kansas prison since being transferred there from the Arkansas state prison system. He had requested the move to be closer to family, who at the time of his request lived in Kansas. His brother, a Rogers businessman, visits him often.

CHAPTER FORTY-ONE

By the summer of 1982, with Perry sentenced to death and Anderson serving a life sentence, the Staton family breathed a little easier. Karen was engaged to be married to a young Van Buren attorney, Frank Booth, and Elaine was going to have another baby in September. Janet and her family were still in Paris, Texas, and doing fine.

But when Karen Staton arrived at the jewelry store on Tuesday morning, July 27th, she discovered that the store had been broken into again. Not knowing if her mother was still home or not, she frantically ran to Gunn-Watts Drug Store and asked the pharmacist, Chuck Watts, to call her mom and see if she answered.

"I'm so scared, I don't think I can dial the number," Karen said.

Watts was a dear friend and had memorized the Staton's number. His heart was beating fast as he listened to each ring.

Finally, the phone was answered.

"Hello," Ruth said.

"Thank God, Ruth. The store's been robbed again."

"Oh, Lord! Is Karen all right?"

Ruth remembered the pictures she had seen of her daughter and husband lying in pools of blood. Was Karen dead on the floor?

Richard Anderson with Sheriff Trellon Ball
...murder suspect talked to reporters Thursday
(SWTR photo by Bill Hayes)

SHERIFF TRELLON BALL ESCORTS RICHARD ANDERSON TO COURT

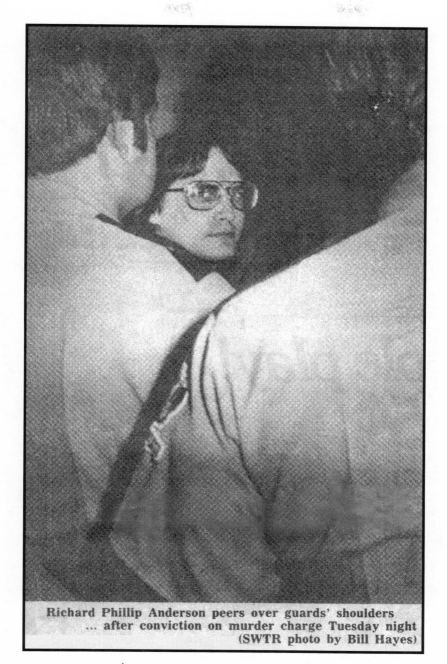

Richard Phillip Anderson peers over guards' shoulders ... after conviction on murder charge Tuesday night (SWTR photo by Bill Hayes)

ANDERSON SENTENCED TO LIFE

Watts could hear the panic in Ruth's voice.

"Karen's okay. She's standing right beside me. Her first thought was if you were okay."

"I don't think I can go through this again."

"Well, you come on down to my store to be with Karen while I call the police."

"Okay. I was just getting ready to come to work when you called. I'll be there in five minutes."

Karen could hear her mother's answers on the phone, and her knees almost buckled with relief. She sat down in a chair next to the phone and listened as Watts called the police.

Chuck placed his hand on her shoulder.

"They say for you to wait here until they get to the store. Someone could still be in there."

When the police arrived, they discovered that the front door had been pried open by the use of something to twist open the front lock and that the outside and inside alarms were turned off. The two-way mirror was covered with newspapers. Both safes were forced open and their contents stolen, which included all the repair work in one safe and the diamond showcases in the other. The watch showcases were looted as well.

When Ruth Staton arrived, the police were already in the store, and Karen stood on the sidewalk in front, waiting for her mom. Once Karen could see that her mother was really and truly safe, she wanted to burst into tears. But her resolve and determination kept her from crying. It was the Staton stoic way to react to adversity.

After walking around the store and seeing the piles of debris and cement left from the prying open of the doors and the damage to the safes, her mother said, "I don't see how we can go through this again."

"Oh, Mother, we've been through a lot worse. We should just thank God that no one was hurt."

Ruth knew that their repair business was brisk, and it was what kept the business afloat in slow months, which were traditionally in the summer.

"But what about the repairs?"

"We have faithful customers. They will be understanding. I've kept good records, and we'll be able to replace those things. It just may take longer."

"I don't know, Karen. I don't know."

"Mother, we have to."

Ruth was acutely aware of the policemen gathering information around the store. She did not want to break down in front of them.

"Okay, if you think we can do it."

"I'll notify the insurance company, and then we'll get this place cleaned up."

What Ruth and Karen did not know was that Eugene Wallace Perry had returned to Fort Smith that same day for a two-hour hearing in Sebastian County Court as part of an appeal to the Arkansas Supreme Court.

A picture appeared the next day in the newspaper of him wearing a three piece suit and being escorted by Sheriff Trellon Ball. His attorneys said that, in going over the transcript of the trial, they had found a statement attributed to Ron Fields that could be construed as being prejudicial to their client. Fields said that Wylie Brewer, Judge Partain's court reporter, had simply misquoted him. Ultimately, the court dismissed Perry's appeal, but it was the first of many hearings that kept the Staton family reliving the murders of Kenneth and Suzanne—and sometimes having to testify during the appeals that kept Perry alive for seventeen years.

Did Perry have something to do with the second robbery? Was he trying to get back at the Statons, and did he have some of his cronies commit the robbery? Or was it just a coincidence? The robbers were never caught, but the police thought they were professional and had ties to Tennessee. And no one ever knew for sure if Perry had anything to do with it.

Cloverleaf Speed Wash was also robbed of cash in their safe that same night. Officers took fingerprints at both places and believed the burglaries were committed by the same people. Police also speculated that the robbery of a safe inside the Safeway grocery store two months earlier might have had a connection to the two robberies across the highway in Cloverleaf Plaza.

The only customer who had left jewelry at Staton's to be repaired and caused any trouble was a woman who claimed she had left a ten thousand dollar ring there. Because of Karen's meticulous record-keeping, she knew the woman was lying. But the woman filed a lawsuit against the jewelry store, which sickened Karen—to think someone would try to take advantage of them that way. The case was resolved after the woman failed a lie detector test and dropped the suit.

Karen had a new, updated alarm system installed, and a new torch and tool resistant safe was placed, this time, in the front of the store. If anyone ever broke into a safe again, they'd be doing it in plain sight.

"With the grace of God," Karen said, "we've made it again."

CHAPTER FORTY-TWO

Marion Pruitt, alias "Mad Dog" Pruitt, a North Carolina native, was a habitual criminal who had been serving a sentence for bank robbery and attempted escape in the Atlanta Federal Penitentiary when his cellmate (a government informant) was murdered. If he agreed to testify concerning the death of his cellmate, the Federal government would parole him with a new name, Charles "Sonny" Pearson, and place him in the Witness Protection Program to receive a monthly stipend and a mobile home in which to live. In 1978, he was resettled to Albuquerque, New Mexico, and when his girlfriend, who later became his wife, joined him, she, too, was put under the Witness Protection Program. Two years later, they were dropped from the program because he had become self-sufficient in a dump truck business.

In 1981, his wife was found in a field, bludgeoned with a hammer and burned. Mad Dog was missing, and he subsequently went on a crime spree of robberies and murders across four states. He killed a bank teller during a robbery in Mississippi, another bank employee in Alabama, moved on to Louisiana to rob a savings and loan bank, and stopped in Fort Smith, Arkansas.

In the early morning hours of October 12th, 1981, he had abducted and murdered Bobbie Jean Roam Robertson, a convenience store worker at a store on Greenwood Road in Fort Smith. Her body was discovered that afternoon, lying facing down in a wooded area along Cliff Drive, less than a mile from the convenience store.

In one of the very first so-called "interstate killings," Mad Dog went on to murder two men in Colorado because, as he told authorities, "I was high on drugs and just wanted to murder somebody . . . like a crazy dog would do."

Mad Dog was eventually caught and convicted in all the states in which the murders took place, but after years of appeals and death penalty overturns, Arkansas was the state in which he was eventually scheduled for execution at the Tucker Unit of the Arkansas penitentiary, where he was returned in 1988.

There, he met Eugene Perry on Death Row.

Perry and Mad Dog reached an agreement. Perry was on death row for only two murders in 1980, crimes he never admitted to. Mad Dog had already admitted killing the Robertson woman in Fort Smith in 1981, which placed him in Arkansas during the same time frame. Mad Dog agreed to say that he and Rick Anderson had known each other a long time, and that they committed the Staton robbery and murders, and Perry was simply the man who was their fence in Atlanta.

Mad Dog was after money. He found a New Mexico attorney, Brian Willett, who brokered a contract with an author who was going to write the life story of Mad Dog. The more murders he had committed and told about, the more vicious and worthy of being immortalized in words he would be. He was even featured on *ABC World News Tonight* with Peter Jennings about the federal witness protection program, which was at that time a $60,000,000 a year program. He tried to extort money from newspapers for exclusive stories, victims' relatives, and anyone he thought might pay him money or "Harley Parts," as he called cash.

Eugene Wallace Perry told Mad Dog specific details about the Staton murders, and Mad Dog confessed in a letter to Willett that he had robbed the jewelry store in Van Buren and killed the father and daughter. He claimed that a man named "Sundance" planned the robbery and "Sportster Rick" assisted him. Mad Dog said he told Anderson, if he didn't name Perry as his partner, he would have his girlfriend and sister killed. He also explained in his letter to Willett that, "My conscience has been bothering me a little, but that doesn't mean I'm going to confess in court."

Willett turned the letters over to Perry's court-appointed attorney, Sam Heuer of Little Rock, who had almost exhausted Perry's tries to avoid the death penalty.

Mad Dog Pruitt's confession automatically gave Perry another chance to appeal his conviction.

CHAPTER FORTY-THREE

In October 1992, Judge Eisele heard the testimony of Eugene Wallace Perry, who appeared with a dark beard and his dark hair pulled back in a ponytail. In a litany of almost comical testimony, Perry tried to prove that he had never even been in Arkansas; he had never met Rick Anderson until he met him in Atlanta and just happened to be with him in Jacksonville, Florida; he had friends with whom he rode motorcycles who knew Damon Peterson and called him "Sundance"; and Sundance's old woman was really Pat Etier, and she ratted on Peterson because she was jealous. Because he was trying to explain the facts to coincide with what Mad Dog Pruitt had told Willett, he often had to change a story in mid-sentence and refer to his notes.

Mad Dog Pruitt refused to testify on the stand because he knew he would be caught up in lies when he was cross-examined.

Ruth Staton Morrison had by this time remarried a university professor, who lived in the state of Washington. She had moved there with him, but after only one year of marriage, he'd suddenly died, and she once again became a widow and eventually returned to Van Buren. She came to Little Rock to testify. So did her daughter, Karen Staton Booth.

Ruth testified that she picked out Perry in a line-up as the man who she waited on, along with Cindy Sue Brown, at the jewelry store a week before it was robbed, and that the ring Perry was wearing when he was arrested in Florida was the ring she had given her husband for their twenty-fifth anniversary.

Karen testified that the jewelry found in Perry's possession was part of the jewelry store's inventory. Price tags in her handwriting were found in the pop-up trailer and old blue Cadillac.

Chantina Ginn testified that she was with Anderson at a Beaver Lake campground when they first met Perry.

Pat Etier testified that she met both Anderson and Perry in a Walmart parking lot, that she laughed her ass off when Perry took off his helmet and his wig came off with it, and that she spent the night with Perry and had sex with him.

Mad Dog's admission was riddled with holes. He was, in reality, being interviewed in New Mexico by an FBI agent on the day of September 10th, 1980. Eye witnesses identified Perry (not Mad Dog) as the man who accompanied Anderson. Eye witnesses placed Perry (not Mad Dog) as the man who bought the Plymouth and rented the storage building.

Mad Dog claimed that Damon Peterson, alias Sundance, was murdered, burned, and buried with the .22 he used to kill the Statons. He claimed Peterson was buried somewhere along the Rio Grande. He also gave a detailed description of Suzanne's breasts and the dress she wore when he killed her and her father (the details were wrong). Mad Dog figured that if Perry was executed when he was really innocent his story would make Arkansas's legal system look bad. He thought that would raise the stakes on his tale of his career as a mass murderer.

Finally, three years later, in March of 1995, Judge Eisele officially concluded that there was no claim to Mr. Perry's innocence based upon unsworn statements of Mr. Pruitt.

Perry appealed the denial of that decision, and once again the Statons were asked to attend another hearing in Little Rock on February 27th, 1997. This time, Elaine Barham brought her son with her and her mom and sister. Kenley, the youngest of Elaine's three boys, had expressed an interest in going, so Elaine had allowed him to make the trip.

Once again, the brave woman from Graphic, Arkansas, Pat Etier, testified. The Statons very much admired this woman because she was the one person who, despite the danger involved in doing so, came forth the day after the robbery to tell the police what she knew about two men she'd drunk beer with at the Terry Motel.

When Ruth reached out to embrace Pat Etier, she recoiled.

"I thought you'd hate me," Pat said.

"Why would you think that? Those men would never have been found if it weren't for you. My family is grateful."

Once again, Perry lost another appeal.

Almost a full seventeen years had passed since the fateful day of September 10th, 1980. It seemed the family would not be able to put their tragedy to rest until Eugene Wallace Perry was dead, and that seemed like it would never happen. Elaine had often said that she dreaded looking at the newspaper because she didn't know when she'd see another article about another appeal.

CHAPTER FORTY-FOUR

In July of 1997, Eugene Wallace Perry lost an appeal to stop his August 6th, 1997, execution date. He had asked Governor Mike Huckabee to grant executive clemency.

The Post Prison Transfer Board had already heard testimony from Perry and his family begging for leniency, claiming that he was a victim of mistaken identity and that he was in another state at the time of the Van Buren robbery and murders. The board also heard emotional testimony from two members of the victims' families: Ruth Staton Morrison, the mother and wife of Suzanne and Kenneth Staton, and Rita Gray, the sister of Kenneth Staton.

Despite her stoic resolve over the years, Ruth Staton Morrison often broke into tears describing the brutal slayings of her husband and daughter, who offered no resistance during the robbery. She told of how her husband had developed crippling rheumatoid arthritis in his early twenties and had worked hard to make their jewelry business a profitable one for them and their four daughters. She said her daughter only weighed one hundred pounds and had just celebrated her twenty-fourth birthday before she was killed. Suzanne had ambitions to become a vet.

Rita Gray, Kenneth Staton's youngest sister, said her brother was a quiet, decent man. She read letters from other family members pleading with the board not to reduce Perry's sentence to life imprisonment. Also testifying was Ron Fields, who urged the board to ignore Perry's claims of mistaken identity and stressed that Perry was a master of disguise. Fields said there were eighty-eight pieces of evidence that tied Perry to the murders.

It took the board less than fifteen minutes to recommend that Governor Huckabee reject Perry's request for executive clemency. Huckabee had previously said that he would abide by the board's final decision, and he did.

CHAPTER FORTY-FIVE

For a man who killed so easily, Eugene Wallace Perry was a man who did not want to die. He continued, through yet another attorney, Craig Lambert, to exhaust all appeals left. They continued to play the Mad Dog Pruitt card, but the phony confession of a multiple murderer was impossible to believe, even if the stars could be lined up in perfect order throughout the galaxy.

The jig was up.

The fat lady had sung.

Perry's date with death was Wednesday, August 6th, 1997.

On Monday, August 4, Perry was escorted by prison guards to the Cummins Unit in Varner, about eighty miles southeast of Little Rock. He was allowed to set up a small statue of Buddha. He had been practicing Buddhism for a year.

On Tuesday and most of the day on Wednesday, he talked on the phone with his mother in Alabama and his daughter, Dawn Perry. He meditated and sang with his spiritual advisor. He sobbed. He requested a thin crust pizza, banana pudding with meringue topping, peanut M&M's, and root beer for his last meal. It took him close to three hours to finish it.

At 8:48 p.m., Perry was transferred to the death chamber and a team of people tied him down to a steel gurney and inserted needles into his arm.

At 9:01 p.m., he recited a Buddhist chant and said, "I am innocent of this crime, and I take refuge in Buddha." He then sang another chant which translated means "the jewel has just left the lotus."

At 9:02 p.m., the injection of chemicals was given. His eyes twitched, his chest heaved twice, his head moved slightly forward. His fingers coiled and turned a grayish-blue. His face went purplish red and then went pale.

At 9:12 p.m., he was pronounced dead.

⁎ ⁎ ⁎ ⁎ ⁎ ⁎

Ruth Staton Morrison and four other family members were allowed to watch over a closed circuit television. Doyle Staton, Kenneth's brother, came from Iowa; his niece Mary Jane came from Missouri; his sister Audrey lived in Fort Smith. They all met at Ruth's house and drove together down to the prison. Elaine's husband, Bill Barham, took a day off work and drove down alone.

At Elaine's house in Van Buren, her three boys had friends over and spent most of the time outdoors, but they were all aware of the event that was happening at the prison. Elaine sat in her living room with Cathy Ulrich, who, along with her husband, Tom, were ministers at the Central Presbyterian Church. Even though Cathy was opposed to the death sentence, she still chose to come to her friend Elaine's home to offer comfort to her and her boys.

"Hey, let's take a ride," she said. "It's so nice outside. Sort of feels like fall."

Elaine sat on the passenger side while Cathy drove along the hilly streets of Van Buren to the city park, where they saw families picnicking by the lake, enjoying the last summer days before school started again.

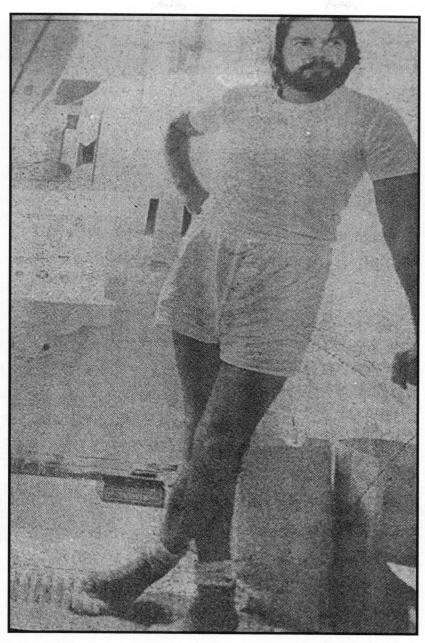

EUGENE WALLACE PERRY ON DEATH ROW. COURTESY OF
FORT SMITH TIMES RECORD, NOVEMBER 14, 1981.

RICHARD ANDERSON, 2016, EL DORADO,
KANSAS, DEPARTMENT OF CORRECTION FACILITY INMATE

"The seasons change. Just like our lives," Cathy said. "But in a predictable way."

Cathy was tall and blonde, while Elaine was a petite brunette. The differences in their looks, just like their own personal beliefs in the death penalty, did not interfere with their friendship. After thirty minutes or so, and a stop at the Sonic Drive-In for a Coke, they returned to Elaine's home.

Karen and a good friend had gone out to eat and had stopped by Elaine's. They were visiting with the youngest boy, Kenley, who was thirteen. They stayed a while, discussing everything but what was going to happen in a couple of hours.

Janet called from Denver, where she and her family now lived. After the phone was passed around to say hellos, they hung up. Cathy left. Then Karen and her friend left.

Elaine remained in the living room, and her boys joined her to wait on the news that the man who killed her daddy and sister was dead.

* * * * * *

Ruth Staton Morrison broke down and sobbed the minute Perry was pronounced dead. After she had composed herself, she talked to the reporters, who had gathered outside Cummins Prison at Varner. She said she hoped no other families would have to go through what hers did for so long.

"I feel justice was served, although very sadly it took seventeen years."

Ruth said she felt for Perry's family, but his execution was tame compared to what he did to her husband and daughter.

"Tonight wasn't as bad as what Suzanne had to watch. He forced Suzanne to watch as her father was shot, all the time knowing that she was next."

Ruth and her in-laws drove home in silence. It had been a grueling day, and there was no need for conversation. It was cloudy that

Wednesday night, and for an August evening, it was cool, with the temperature in the mid-sixties. Not at all like that horribly hot summer of 1980.

Maybe that's a good sign, Ruth thought. *Maybe that's a good sign.*

—THE END—

EPILOGUE

This was written shortly before Kenley Barham's untimely death on Thanksgiving, November 24th, 2016, at the age of thirty-two.

* * * * * *

Beyond Tragedy
by Kenley Barham

I never met my grandfather, and I never met the woman who would have become my aunt. On September 10th, 1980, two men armed with pistols and staunch determination proceeded to carry out a malevolent plan. In mere minutes, not only had the lives of two beloved individuals been taken, but a wake of grief had already begun to take root, waiting in earnest to envelope those closest to Suzanne and Kenneth in an inescapable cocoon of terminal despair.

Misery swirled all around them, but each member of my family possessed a powerful resolve, one made even more formidable by the intense bond they had always shared. It was this bond that not only allowed them to recover from such an unexpected loss, but it gave them back the grit that had allowed them to push aside doubt and succeed in the first place. Despite the tragedy that occurred on that smoldering day in September, my family has managed to spend the last thirty-six years of their lives outside the wasteland of anguish, where only thoughts of desolation manage to take root. Instead, they chose to move forward in a positive manner, confident that the intense bond and unyielding resolve unique to the Staton family would carry them.

When my mother entered the store on that fateful evening, she must have had some idea of what was to be found in that back room, yet she entered the room anyway. Because fear of what you *will* find is always trumped by the hope of what you *might* find.

My mother has never told me the story of walking into that room and finding her father and sister bound, gagged, and each shot twice in the head. She has never told me of how she believed they might still be alive, and that if she screamed loud enough at them to wake up they might do just that. She has never told me of how she desperately tried to remove their binding and gags while begging for them to show any sign of life. This lasted until the police arrived and drug her from the room where the two people she loved most in the world had both drawn their last breaths.

I can tell you this: every time that story is brought up, the haunted look in her eyes is unmistakable. In that instance, she is no longer in the room with me; she is reliving that horrific series of events as if she is once again in that exact moment. Seeing her like that, reliving events I can't even imagine experiencing, squeezes my heart, steals my breath, and blurs my vision. This happens every time the subject is brought up, and every time I am racked with sadness, seeing my mom going through such pain, and knowing she will never fully escape that pain because she will never escape that memory—that moment—the worst of her life.

My family chose to carry on as a testimony to the legacy of their lost loved ones. Each was able to take his or her damaged willpower and combine it into a force potent enough to do just that almost immediately after the murder of my grandfather Kenneth and my aunt Suzanne. I can think of no illustration that better defines this family's love for each other and the staunch determination that the memory of both Kenneth and Suzanne would never fade.

Since I have no personal memories of either Kenneth or Suzanne, I've tapped into the memories of those who did know them and in a way feel that I remember them by proxy. The consensus from those who knew Kenneth is that he was both quiet and patient, but he was also a man of determination with a willingness to do anything it took to care for his family, even after being stricken with crippling arthritis, the onset of which seemed especially cruel for a man like Kenneth who loved and excelled at outside activities such as hunting and fishing, the type of twelve-year-old kid who picked green beans until he saved up just enough money to buy a used bicycle.

He was a man determined to open his own jewelry business despite being constantly riddled with pain and confined to a wheelchair. For years he had been unable to work; his wife Ruth worked nights at Dixie Cup in Fort Smith in order to support the family. He loved his family, and he was determined to do whatever it took to remove the financial burden from his wife. After taking a watch repair class, and with the astronomical support of his wife and others, he did just that. He ran a highly respected jewelry store with the help of his wife and two of his daughters—Karen and Suzanne.[2]

Because Kenneth was often confined to the family home, he spent more time with his daughters than many other fathers, allowing him to forge a personal bond more powerful than many other patriarchs. In an effort to teach Karen how to tell time, he promised her a watch. That was incentive enough, and so by the time she was in the second grade, she owned her very own watch.

Janet seemed to naturally gravitate toward the boundless parameters of the written word, and Kenneth spent many hours helping to foster her love of fiction. My mother, unfortunately, inherited his arthritis, so a special bond was formed between the two. They both had a deep

---

[2] Kenneth did have times when he was in a really bad way, or was hospitalized after surgery, and Ruth worked to support the family, but he worked when he could.

understanding of what the other was going through. Only they could understand how a constant agony might begin to seem normal after a certain amount of time had passed.

When Suzanne was young, she often wanted to sit in her dad's lap. Her mom discouraged it, but Kenneth always obliged, despite the pain. There simply wasn't enough agony available to force Kenneth into concession with the love he had for his family.

I desperately wish I had known my grandfather.

Unfortunately, I know much less about Suzanne, a fact that brings with it great sadness. However, make no mistake: the fact that I was less successful at getting others to conjure up specific memories of Suzanne is in no way an indication that she was a less crucial or important member of this family. In fact, I view a lack of specific memories as a positive in Suzanne's case. It's the flamboyant and dramatic events of the past that we often remember the most. A lack of specifics in Suzanne's case is simply a reflection of her character. Suzanne was smart, kind, soft-spoken, and a bit introverted. These are not the traits of someone desperate to stand out in a crowd. I do know that, like my mother, she harbored a deep affection for animals. In her case, it was a basset hound named Pearl that she loved dearly. Her husband, Tom, was a musician, so he spent much of his time at the studio recording or out on tour. This left Suzanne at home alone quite often, and it seems like Pearl was her closest companion. Sometimes she and Tom would take Pearl hiking, and the next day Suzanne would notice that her beloved dog just didn't seem as tirelessly energetic as usual. She liked to comically attribute this lethargy to Pearl's short legs, absurdly choosing to ignore the idea that her cherished pet's exhaustion was simply due to a lengthy travel she was unaccustomed to.

Because Suzanne and my mom were best friends, I can't think of a better way to encapsulate Suzanne's legacy than with a story my mom told me. When my oldest brother Ben was born in 1978, Suzanne desperately wanted to be there. Unfortunately, my mom gave birth in

Fayetteville, Arkansas, while Suzanne was stuck in Van Buren, which meant her only way to take part in this special event was through a phone call to my mother. In tears, the last thing she said to my mom before hanging up was, "You know, I don't think there's anyone else in the world who loves you more than me."

With the overwhelming support of both her loved ones and an abundance of people she had never met, Ruth's steely resolve gradually began to return. She received thousands of cards and donations from friends, family, and even strangers separated by such distances as Spain, Saudi Arabia, and Africa. She even received a hand-written letter of condolence from the man who was governor of Arkansas at the time: Bill Clinton.

She continued to work at Staton's Jewelry after its reopening in 1980, but only when she wasn't spending the majority of her time advocating for victims' rights. In 1985, she was introduced to Kenneth Morrison, a man who had relatives in Van Buren. Shortly thereafter, the two married and moved to Pullman, Washington. Sadly, Kenneth died of a heart attack a year later.

Despite now living alone and away from her family, Ruth had made a name for herself and acquired a substantial number of friends, so she decided to stay in Pullman for the time being. During that time she was encouraged to partake in a number of city functions where she naturally excelled. Because she had acquired such a stellar reputation, a number of people encouraged her to run for the position of Precinct Chairperson. Another man was running for the position, and many people believed that his plans for change would cause irreparable damage to the town. Ruth agreed, and after joining the campaign, she won in a landslide.

Fortunately, she decided it was time to move back to Arkansas in 1993, where most of her family still lived. Here in her home state was her greatest accomplishment of all: sharing with us the boundless joy, wisdom, charity, and knowledge that she possesses. Without her guidance over the past two decades, I would be a much different person than the man I am today.

Very soon after the murders, my Aunt Karen made a bold and brave choice that perhaps had the most vital impact on my family's mental state at the time—a choice that brought my family together in a positive way and, most importantly, gave them a glimpse of a possible future where each person might not forever live in the shadows of grief and despair. Her decision: reopen Staton's Jewelry. As expected, this came as a shock to everyone in the family, especially considering the murders had occurred only a few days prior. Nobody wanted to walk back into that store so soon, or ever again for that matter. But Karen would not waver because the store was their livelihood.

But I suspect that Karen had another reason for wanting to reenter the store so soon after the murders. Whether intentionally or subconsciously, she knew that bringing everyone back to the place that defined the Staton legacy—and also stood as a testament to the kind of man Kenneth Staton was, a man of unwavering determination who was willing to endure unimaginable pain in order to open his own business and provide for his family—would have a binding effect, allowing each individual to share what little reserve they had left at a time when they needed each other the most. Very slowly, every member of the Staton family came back to the store, allowing each individual however much time was needed to reintegrate themselves with a place that had long served as a monument for what the Staton name stood for. As everyone regained some semblance of normality after continuing to work together, those thin tendrils of willpower that had previously barely prevented collapse began to grow thicker, a brightly lit oval of sinew that enabled each family member to push back against the grief that had so recently pounced upon them.

Though the store no longer stands today (Karen kept the store open and the family name in the public eye until ultimately closing in 1998), I believe it was this bond that has energized this family and allowed us to remain close, despite the inevitable adversity that often rips other families apart. In essence, if not for Karen's resolve, I almost certainly would not be putting these words to page at this very moment. For that, I thank her.

Of the three remaining sisters, I would describe Janet as the most enigmatic. This is not an insult, by any means. In fact, I always felt that it was one of her most enduring qualities. You could never quite place your finger on what she was thinking, but you were always sure that an intricate series of rapidly moving cogs ceaselessly spun within her mind. Sometimes she would sit for long stretches in silent contemplation; at other times, she would unexpectedly speak at length about a myriad of different topics. Fortunately, those topics where never boring. Though she lived miles away in Colorado, I always felt that she and I shared a special kind of bond. When I was roughly twelve years old, I became an avid reader of fiction, much as Janet had when she was a child. We both shared a love of Stephen King novels, and to this day, every time I pick up his newest book, I immediately think of her.

She even owned a Super Nintendo and was an avid player of video games. That an adult loved to play video games might seem like a given to a more modern generation, but in the early 1990s video games were exclusively for children; most adults at time probably viewed the act of picking up a game controller on par with building doll houses or playing with G. I. Joes. I constantly anticipated my family's frequent trips to Colorado, hoping Janet would finally show me how to obtain a 100% completion rating in Super Mario World. (Trust me, it's a revered accomplishment.) As Janet and her husband, Tommy, grew older, they decided to move back to more familiar territory in Fort Smith. Sadly, Janet unexpectedly passed away a few years later.

My mother made me promise not to play favorites and depict her as some kind of saint. I promised I would not. However, because *she is in fact my mother*, I'm sure I will find myself unwittingly breaking that promise.

Over the course of many decades, she has been a dedicated member of Central Presbyterian Church in Fort Smith. She has repeatedly

191

served as a deacon and elder, many times as the treasurer. She is also deeply involved in the CE Committee. Also, it seems that every other time I call her she is busy making muffins and sack lunches for children who often go without the food we take for granted. However, she insists that giving birth to three boys and raising them into respectful, successful, self-reliant young men is her greatest accomplishment.

Finally, I promised that when writing about my mom I would not heap praise upon her by telling of her myriad accomplishments, by speaking of all the obstacles she has had to navigate and the hurdles she's had to leap. I promised not to write about all the struggles and strife she has endured throughout her life while still ensuring that her three boys were raised properly. Such a description might possibly conjure a saintly image. So I will simply tell the truth: she is the kindest, toughest, most compassionate, bravest, most loyal, protective, and sweetest person I have ever known. In short, she has been the greatest mom in the world. I realize there may be a few people who disagree with that statement, but I challenge them to spend no more than five minutes in her presence before pulling out their phones to apologize to their own mothers for the inevitable truth they have just learned.

I believe that the good in this world vastly outweighs the bad. Maybe I can't prove it, but I do know this: despair will always exist, but so will kindness, compassion, love, acclimation, resolution, and eventually . . . comfort.

If there is only one person in this world who truly knows the meaning of the word despair, it is certainly my grandmother Ruth. She has faced it and continued to live her life on her own terms. She has been able to do this because she knows that despair is consistently outmatched by the good in this world.

Such goodness is plainly evident through the words spoken by my grandmother in the wake of Eugene Wallace Perry's execution: "Again I wept and forgave him. I try not to think about where he is spending eternity. God knows."

ACKNOWLEDGEMENTS

I first want to thank Paul Guiffre for being my best friend and a brilliant attorney, who guided me through the awful years following my husband's death. I will forever be grateful.

Thanks to Duke, Kimberly, Kelsey and Meg of Pen-L Publishing for shaping this into a book I'm proud of.

For almost a year, Ruth Staton Morrison, Karen Staton Farmer, Elaine Staton Barham, and Kenley Barham met with me on Sunday afternoons. As we sat around Karen's dining room table and looked out on the majestic view of the Arkansas River, they once again traveled along that awful road that began on September 10th, 1980. Each warmly welcomed me and answered my questions, no matter how sadly difficult they were. Because of their loving presence, I now feel that I am part of their family (although I cry much easier that they do).

Thanks to Bill and Ginny Womble for their genuine interest and help on this book. Cheerleaders, they were and are.

The Fort Smith Public Library, particularly the director, Jennifer Goodson, and the endowment chairman, Cindy Long, have been my biggest supporters. They made wonderful things happen following the publication of my first book, *Blind Rage*.

Thanks also to my daughter, Jennifer Paddock, who shares her knowledge of writing and books with me and never fails to make me laugh. She and her brothers, David X Williams and Brady Paddock, have heaped praises on my shoulders and convinced me that maybe I am a real writer after all.

Betty Christian was always ready for a speaking trip, be it Little Rock or Checotah, Oklahoma. Bob and Nadine Miller bought more *Blind Rage* books than anyone, including my faithful friends Tom and Lorna Pryor, Eleanor Clark, Peggy Weidman, Doug and Jan Kelley, Dixie Kline, Katy Boulden, P.D. DuVall, Carol Mason, and Jay Willis, who were overly generous in their support. The whippersnapper, Christina Scherrey, was her usual helpful self.

Thanks also to Richard Anderson who, once I told him I was writing the story of the Staton Jewelry Store robbery and murders with the blessings of the family, willingly shared his past with me. He prays the Staton family will one day be able to forgive him. Thanks also to his brother, Bryan, who exemplifies the term "brotherly love."

And thanks to the book clubs who invited me into their living rooms and libraries and made me feel like a rock star and to those who bought *Blind Rage* and told their friends about it.

I hope you'll feel the same way about *Closing Time.*

ABOUT THE AUTHOR

Anita Paddock is a life-long resident of the Van Buren-Fort Smith, Arkansas, area. The widowed mother of two grown children, she has spent 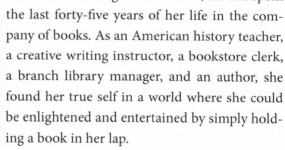 the last forty-five years of her life in the company of books. As an American history teacher, a creative writing instructor, a bookstore clerk, a branch library manager, and an author, she found her true self in a world where she could be enlightened and entertained by simply holding a book in her lap.

While researching her first true crime novel, *Blind Rage*, she realized that there had been other murders during 1980 and 1981 in Van Buren and its neighboring city, Fort Smith. Since both towns were part of the same judicial district, law enforcement officers and prosecutors had scrambled to solve the crimes committed during the period they called "The Summers of Death."

Closing Time tells the horrific story of another one of those crimes.

FIND ANITA AT:
Facebook: Anita.Paddock
Website: www.AnitaPaddock.com

BLIND RAGE

BY ANITA PADDOCK

**A true story of sin, sex, and murder
in a small Arkansas town.
Who did it and why will shock you.**

CHAPTER ONE

May 16, 1981

Ruie Ann Park glanced at herself in the bathroom mirror. Her head was covered with thirty pin curls held in place by thirty bobby pins. On her chest were red splotches, sure signs she was angry. She grabbed her pink nylon robe from the hook behind the door and threw it over her matching nightgown with an exaggerated motion that made the robe fan out in a half-circle. Joan Crawford had donned a robe with the same flair in one of her early gangster movies, *The Damned Don't Cry*, and Ruie Ann thought she favored the movie star.

She returned to the guest room and sat on the bed, crossing her arms over sagging breasts, impatiently waiting for the apology that never came. Instead, she felt the first of ten hacking blows to the top of her head and left temple. She screamed and struggled to fend off the attacker, grabbing hands, hair. Blood spurted and ran down her face and onto her neck and chest.

She fought hard and broke two fingers on her left hand and cut her right. She fell over onto the foot of the bed, soaking the mattress with blood. And then she felt hands around her ankles.

She was dragged off the mattress, face down across the hard floor, down the hallway, and across a rug that bunched under her. She raised her left arm, knocking books from a shelf in the den. Finally, she lay still, the metallic scent of the blood pooling under her head filling her nostrils. She felt something thrown over her, and seconds later, she heard the den door open and quietly close.

At first, the seventy-five-year-old widow didn't realize how badly she was injured, but she could feel the sticky blood on her neck and arms. Her head throbbed worse than any migraine she'd ever had, and when she tried to lift it, she couldn't. Her throat was dry, and she wished for a sip of water. Minutes passed before she lost consciousness, and her last thoughts were of how she would ever get rid of the blood stains in the showplace of Van Buren, Arkansas.

FIND THE REST OF THE STORY AT
WWW.PEN-L.COM/BLINDRAGE.HTML

Dear Readers,
If you enjoyed this book enough to review it for Goodreads, B&N, or Amazon.com, I'd appreciate it!
Thanks, Anita

Find more great reads at
Pen-L.com

Made in the USA
Columbia, SC
23 June 2020